John Wesley, Natural Man,
and the 'Isms'

John Wesley, Natural Man, and the 'Isms'

J. ROBERT EWBANK

RESOURCE *Publications* · Eugene, Oregon

JOHN WESLEY, NATURAL MAN, AND THE 'ISMS'

Resource Publications
A Division of Wipf and Stock Publishers
199 W. 8th Ave., Suite 3
Eugene, OR 97401

www.wipfandstock.com

ISBN 13: 978-1-49825-339-0

Manufactured in the U.S.A.

Unless otherwise stated, Scripture quotations are from the King James Version of the Bible.

This book is dedicated to John and Mattie,
Colin, William and Philip, and Helen and Betty.

Contents

Preface ix
Acknowledgments xi
Introduction xiii

1 Natural Man and Prevenient Grace 1

2 Heathenism, Indians, and Christianity 17

3 Judaism and Christianity 35

4 Deism and "True Christianity" 51

5 Roman Catholicism and "True Christianity" 68

6 Quakerism and "True Christianity" 94

7 Mysticism and "True Christianity" 111

8 Conclusion 133

Study Guide 147
Bibliography 177

Preface

THIS BOOK WAS WRITTEN out of a love for John Wesley and his theology. He is one of the most amazing Christian men the world has ever seen. The number of books he wrote and the number of books he abbreviated for the people of England is absolutely amazing. All this, combined with a staggering amount of preaching, make his contribution to Christian thought and practice one of the greatest of all the Protestant Reformers.

Many have written about the core of John Wesley's theology, the Order of Salvation. Comments have been made within this book and its bibliography recommending some good books one might want to read about this topic.

This book is about John Wesley's dealings with religions outside Christianity, including several he considers to be distortions of Christianity. We lay a background of prevenient grace, which is a Wesleyan way of avoiding the problems of Calvinism and Pelagianism.

Our study continues with a discussion of Heathenism and Wesley's earlier wrong thinking about the American Indians.

Then we discuss Judaism, the ground from which Christianity grew. Judaism and Christianity share a closeness they do not have with other religions.

We move then to some of the distortions of Christianity with which Wesley deals, including Deism, Roman Catholicism, Mysticism, and Quakerism.

Our study will focus on the differences of these religions or ways of thought compared to Wesley's "True Christianity."

We also will see what Wesley thinks about the possibilities for those who have these other beliefs to be saved by God.

Wesley is a man of "one book," so be prepared for his foundation upon the Scriptures in all of his discussions with those who have different points of view and are not believers in "True Christianity." This is a foundation he never leaves.

Wesley is a fascinating man with theological insights that are suggestive for us today. They can be helpful in our discussions with other religions and others who share the title "Christian." Let us begin.

Acknowledgments

THIS BOOK WOULD NOT exist without the help and support of many who played a part in its creation.

Thanks to my parents, John R. (second generation Methodist minister and college professor) and Mattie Ewbank (teacher and world class encourager of the author) for raising me even though I'm sure it was difficult at times.

The teachers along the way, especially those at Garrett Evangelical Theological Seminary, Evanston, Illinois. With deep appreciation to Dr. William Hordern who created in me a love for theology and Dr. Colin Williams who created in me a love specifically for John Wesley. Also a special thanks to Dr. Philip S. Watson who worked with me on a Masters in the Theology of John Wesley when I returned to Garrett after earning my first Masters Degree. It is with regret that I was unable to finish the program.

Special thanks to Kathleen Kordesh of Garrett Evangelical Theological Seminary who helped me with quotes when due to my own negligence the book or page, or in some cases both, totally escaped me. Also to Martha Wood of Mobile, Alabama, who took her time to valiantly work through the book and offer helpful comments.

Couldn't do without Christian Amondson, Assistant Managing Editor of Wipf and Stock Publishers, who was so helpful, also in providing copyeditor Nancy Shoptaw, who worked word by word through the manuscript with me. A huge thanks to her and to him.

Two spouses need to be thanked. Helen Glenn died after 48 years of matrimony, during which she helped raise our three children, Glenda Sealy, Shawn R. Ewbank, and Todd C. Ewbank. She continually encouraged my work in John Wesley. Sarah "Betty" Brandon has been with me for over five years of happiness, and through whom I am able to know her son Rob Brandon. Without her prodding and encouragement the effort would not have been made to complete this book on John Wesley.

There undoubtedly have been many others along the way. Thanks to one and all.

Introduction

A N INTERESTING QUESTION BEING called to our attention, in these days of the councils of churches and the clashing of Christianity with other world religions, concerns the place of the other religions in relation to Christianity. Is there, in reality, only one religion that is for the total of mankind, or is there a religion for the followers of Christ, for the followers of Judaism, and so forth? In other words, are all religions the same or are there just multitudes of ways of finding the same God, or is there a singular way, that of Christianity? And, if there is only one way to God, what happens to those people who have other beliefs? Is it possible for them to be saved or not?

Christianity itself has proliferated into many different groups over the centuries. Some of these groups are very much alike with only small shades of differences, so small that it is difficult to tell them apart. Others are quite different in their approach. We will study some of these groups and see also what Wesley says about their inclusion in Christianity and the possibility of salvation for their followers.

One may think that this is a modern problem, brought up by the complexities of our modern living and shrinking world, but in reality, it had to be faced from the inception of Christianity into the world. As a monotheistic faith, Christians believe there is but one God and that one God is known in the unique and final revealing of Himself through Jesus Christ, the Son of God. This faith sometimes places us in a peculiar and awkward position as we deal with those of other religious faiths.

Our purpose here is to enter into conversation with John Wesley on these questions. We seek to find whether he thought all religions of equal value for the individual, or if there is something unique and final to be found in Christianity. We will also look at others who believe that they are Christian but do not hold to mainstream Christian teachings. Also, we seek to find out what John Wesley thought about the possibility of salvation for those who believe in the god/God of these other religions.

In dealing with John Wesley, as any great man, we must constantly be on guard against some perils. We must not place Wesley and his thought over Christ. We study Wesley to answer these questions not because he stands in Christ's place, but because he was intimate with Christ, and a great interpreter of Him.

> John Wesley was one of the great churchmen of all times, no doubt about that, but Wesley was great because he exalted Christ.... We study Wesley because he found that power in full measure and in the understanding of him we may find our way to the same source of divine help. We turn to the past, not as those who have no plans for the future, but as those who are seeking the unchanging source of power that we may carry their plans into effect.[1]

As we consider these questions we will look at a variety of persuasions or positions because we are fortunate enough to find materials supporting Wesley's dialogue with them. Some of these positions are not Christian, while others would include themselves within Christianity. The reason for dealing with the latter is that Wesley often thought some within Christianity as far wrong as some who were without.

The positions we will be dealing with are the Heathen, Indians, Jews, Roman Catholics, Deists, Mystics, and Quakers. From the "ism" point of view we are discussing Heathenism, Judaism, Roman Catholicism, Deism, Mysticism, and Quakerism. This gives our study an interesting array of views.

Judaism represents another worldwide religion. Heathen and the Indian, particularly the American Indian, represent two faiths outside of Christianity. We look at a philosophical misunderstanding of Christianity represented by Deism. Finally we will consider those who believe themselves to be Christians, including the Roman Catholics, Mystics, and Quakers.

One might consider other positions that Wesley recognizes as a part of the problem, such as some of the philosophies and philosophers and the case of the Negro. However, such a broadening of our study would bear little new fruit, with the possible exception of the philosophies. Unfortunately there is not enough material to do a complete and realistic study of Islam.

Our primary resource material comes from the writings of John Wesley himself. There is very little material bearing directly on the topic

---

1. Watkins, *Out of Aldersgate*, 7.

found in commentators upon Wesley and no need to look elsewhere, anyway. We will be using the "works," "letters," "journals," "notes," and "hymns" of Wesley. Other materials will supplement the study and can be found in the bibliography.

We are not going to deal with the center of Wesleyan theology, which is the individual's concern for salvation. The core of Wesley's theology is built around the theme of salvation, the many graces of God, and the phases of man's response to God's plan of salvation. These themes form the center of Wesley's thought and life. This theological hub may likewise be found in his lifelong quest for personal salvation, which marked his life as one of major purpose.

We deal with a sidelight from the main center of Wesley's concern of salvation.[2] We are going to focus our discussion upon the study of other religions and their relationship to Christianity, other Christian believers who are much different from "True Christianity," and the possibility of salvation for all of these groups. Again there is precious little secondary material to be found that directly relates to our study. As we study usable material for our topic from Wesley's writings we find that it is not always at the center of his concern, but rather it is often a peripheral topic that he happens to be discussing.

The intense practicality of Wesley's mind is evident in his sermons. He was preaching to people who were Christians, who imagined themselves as Christians, or at least considered themselves to be nominally Christian. His concern was to point out the true path and way of Christianity. He also sought to distinguish between the misconceptions about Christianity and the "True Christianity" that he had found.

As a way of introducing our topic and preparing background material that provides a basic foundation for it, we will consider briefly, Natural Man and *prevenient* or *preventing grace*. This study will then lead us into the topic upon which the book is centered.

Much suggestive and interesting material could be found in a full-scale search into the doctrines of *prevenient* or *preventing grace*, and orthodoxy or right *opinion* versus the living relationship with God. However, such a full-scale study, though interesting, would again lead us astray of our major purpose, which is to determine if there is uniqueness and finality in Christianity as understood by Wesley and to discover the relation of "True Christianity" to some other Christians who Wesley thought were

2. Wesley, *Works*, 6:381.

wide of the mark. Many of these minor themes will find a place in our study, but they are not of major importance for our purposes.

Wesley had a greater concern for *essence* than for the *opinions* of the doctrine.[3] The means or how we interpret a doctrine was not nearly as important for him as the fact that the person believed in the significance of it. In this way he distinguishes between the *fact* and *manner* of a doctrine.

> Now the mystery does not lie in the *fact*, but altogether in the *manner*. For instance: "God said, Let there be light: And there was light." I believe it: I believe the plain *fact*: There is no mystery at all in this. The mystery lies in the *manner* of it. But of this I believe nothing at all; nor does God require it of me.[4]

For those who are interested, Wesley follows this example with two others: the Incarnation and the Trinity. Thus, we see that for Wesley, there are limits to man's knowledge about the doctrines of Christianity. Though the depth of the doctrine's mystery may not be fully plumbed, the fact of the doctrine may and should be known and accepted.

Wesley makes another helpful distinction concerning Christian doctrine. He finds a difference between the basic Christian *doctrines* and theological *opinions*. Some doctrines are basic, and some are only *opinions*. Orthodoxy, or *right opinion*, is not the ultimate in Christian experience. Orthodoxy or *right opinion* may be helpful and important in the interpretation of doctrine, but it is not the sum and total of Christianity. One may hold to the right in *opinion* and be wrong in salvation, yet again; the reverse may equally be true.

> Orthodoxy, I say, or right opinion, is but a slender part of religion at best, and sometimes no part at all. I mean, if a man be a child of God, holy in heart and life, his right opinions are but the smallest part of his religion: if a man be a child of the devil, his right opinions are no part of religion, they cannot be; for he that does the works of the devil has no religion at all.[5]

Opinions are not altogether dismissed, because they are vital, and Wesley certainly had them, and voiced them frequently. Even so he viewed them as only a small part of religion.

3. Wesley, *Standard Sermons*, 2:126–46.

4. Wesley, *Works*, 6:204.

5. Wesley, *Letters*, 3:183.

Now a look must be given to the general outline of the book. It will be evident that it is divided into the large areas of Wesley's thought concerning other religions and the inner corruptions of Christianity.

Each of these areas is divided into the definition of who is under consideration, the failures that they make, the possibilities that they have for salvation, and a short comparison of them with Wesley's "True Christianity."

Most of what we will be discussing is self explanatory, but two things need further clarification. We must define what "salvation" means within the limits of this book. Wesley himself distinguished between two possible definitions. The first means everything in the relationship between God and man that comes from God's grace. All relationships, all callings of God, all benefits of His love, and all of God's merciful dealings with man are included. Wesley defines it in this manner:

> If we take this in its utmost extent, it will include all that is wrought in the soul by what is frequently termed "natural conscience," but more properly, "preventing grace"; all the drawings of the Father— the desires after God, which if we yield to them, increase more and more; all that light wherewith the Son of God, "enlighteneth every one that cometh into the world"—showing every man "to do justly, to love mercy, and to walk humbly with his God"; all the convictions which His Spirit, from time to time, works in every child of man—although it is true, the generality of men stifle them as soon as possible, and after awhile forget, or at least deny, that they ever had them at all.[6]

The second definition consists of the two parts: *justification* and *sanctification. Justification* is understood to be pardon, forgiveness for sins, or our acceptance by God. *Sanctification* is the process of growth in holiness from the time of *justification* to *complete sanctification* or Christian perfection.

> It is thus that we wait for entire sanctification; for a full salvation from all our sins—from pride, self-will, anger, unbelief; or, as the Apostle expresses it, "go on unto perfection . . ." It is love excluding sin; love filling the heart, taking up the whole capacity of the soul. It is love "rejoicing evermore, praying without ceasing, in everything giving thanks."[7]

6. Wesley, *Standard Sermons*, 2:445.
7. Ibid., 2:448.

Another unclear area for now is what Wesley means by "True Christianity." However, this will be more clearly shown as we develop our thinking. A quick and working definition would be the renewal of God's righteousness in us, or the renewal of God's image in us, which is a good Wesleyan definition.

> A restoration of man by Him that bruises the serpent's head, to all that the old serpent deprived him of; a restoration, not only to the favour but likeness to the image of God, implying not barely deliverance from sin, but the being filled with the fullness of God. It is plain, if we attend to the preceding considerations, that nothing short of this is Christian religion.[8]

The Wesleyan doctrines were put to verse by John and Charles Wesley. The message was sung by the common people set to the bar tunes of the day. The Methodist Church was born singing theology. It is therefore easy to understand why there will be many quotes from Wesley's Hymns.

With these things in mind, we are ready to begin with Natural Man and the *prevenient* or *preventing* grace of God that attends him.

8. Wesley, Works, 6:276.

Natural Man and Prevenient Grace

THE CONDITION OF NATURAL MAN

NATURAL MAN IS THE end result of man's separation from God. Man, being born and created in the image of God, has fallen from that image because of his sin. The entire image has not been lost, for there are elements remaining, twisted and distorted though they may be. Wesley believes the image of God is more than a single element. Man's image involves the *natural image*,[1] the *political image*, and the *moral image*.[2] Only the *moral image* suffers total depravity in natural man. The others—natural and political—are warped and indistinct.

> "And God," the three-one God, "said, Let us make man in our image, after our likeness. So God created man in his own image, in the image of God created he him:" (Gen 1: 26–27)—Not barely in his *natural image*, a picture of his own immortality; a spiritual being, endued with understanding, freedom of will, and various affections;—nor merely in his *political image*, the governor of this lower world, having "dominion over the fishes of the sea, and over all the earth;"—but chiefly in his *moral image*; which, according to the Apostle, is "righteousness and true holiness."[3]

Man, as natural man, has suffered the loss of the *moral image*,[4] and the distortion of the others. As a result of the loss of the *moral image*, there is nothing that a human being can do in order to make himself righteous or holy in the eyes of God. Thus, by his own heroic actions, there is nothing

1. Wesley, *Works*, 6:269–70.
2. Ibid., 6:270–71.
3. Ibid., 6:66.
4. Ibid., 6:272.

he can do to restore the broken relationship with his creator. No act of our will, no collection of pure thoughts, no sacrifice—nothing—can re-create us as righteous, fit for the presence of God. Man's nature now is such that he does not have within himself the power to do it.

Wesley declares his position with regard to the nature of man in many of his sermons. However, in his *Journal* he gives us a valuable summary for our consideration. Natural man is in a deplorable condition.

> . . . I declared with all plainness of speech: (1) that, by nature, they were all children of wrath; (2) that all their natural tempers were corrupt and abominable; and (3) all their words and works, which could never be any better but by faith; and that (4) a natural man has no more faith than a devil, if so much.[5]

This outline presents the main and salient points that Wesley maintained through the years. The condition of man is so bad that nothing but the work of God's grace in his heart is able to save man from his sickness.[6] Natural man has no knowledge of God; he has no acquaintanceship with the Creator of his life.[7]

To use another analogy, we might say that natural man is spiritually asleep. Because he is spiritually asleep he is in some sense at rest because there is nothing spiritually to disturb him. Because he is asleep and at rest he is utterly ignorant of his true condition before God. This ignorance of his true condition before God allows natural man to have a false joy, thinking that everything is fine. Due to his ignorance and false joy he has a false liberty in his actions. Believing he is free and able to decide his actions, he is really a servant of sin.[8] We could propose to push the analogy further and say that if he is spiritually asleep maybe he can become spiritually awake. With this thought, however, Wesley would disagree. So much for this analogy, we have pushed it to its limits and perhaps beyond its limits.

The natural man has neither fear nor love,[9] is spiritually dead and close to eternal death,[10] and is at a distance from God.[11] His thoughts wander continually from God.[12] To sum up:

5. Wesley, *Journal*, 3:65.

6. Wesley, *Works*, 7:340.

7. Ibid., 6:59.

8. Ibid., 5:99–101.

9. Wesley, *Notes*, 915.

10. Ibid., 656.

11. Ibid., 16.

12. Wesley, *Standard Sermons*, 2:180–81.

But the natural man—That is, every man who hath not the Spirit; who has no other way of obtaining knowledge, but by his senses and natural understanding. *Receiveth not*—Does not understand or conceive. *The things of the Spirit*—The things revealed by the Spirit of God, whether relating to His nature or His kingdom. *For they are foolishness to him*—He is so far from understanding, that he utterly despises, them. *Neither can he know them*—As he has not the will, so neither has he the power. *Because they are spiritually discerned*—They can only be discerned by the aid of that Spirit, and by those spiritual senses, which he has not.[13]

Natural man has no chance of salvation, for he is separated from the author of salvation. As natural man, God is apart from him, but in reality—in existence as we know it—God is seeking and working within him. As Colin W. Williams writes:

The loss of the moral image spells total depravity because separation from God and the substitution of self-government in place of acceptance or the Lordship of God means that the good capacities of man are twisted from their true course and used for a wrong purpose.[14]

THE REALITY OF NATURAL MAN

Interestingly enough, we find that for all he has written about him, Wesley does not believe in the existence of natural man, per se. Natural man by definition is man completely apart from God, totally separated from Him. This man does not have a saving relationship with God, and is not even pointing or moving in that direction. His mind is set upon this world, and the things to be found therein.

Umphrey Lee writes:

But for Wesley the "natural man" is a logical abstraction. Like the economic man or the caricatures set up today by amateur psychologists, anthropologists, and theologians, the "natural man" does not exist . . . for Wesley, the "natural man" is only a logical fiction.[15]

In our previous discussion of natural man, we seemed to find quite a bit of life within him. Though he partakes of logical reality, he has no

---

13. Wesley, *Notes*, 591.

14. Williams, *John Wesley's Theology Today*, 49.

15. Lee, *Wesley and Modern Religion*, 124–25.

flesh and blood counterpart in real life. Wesley answers this problem by declaring, in his sermon "Working Out Our Own Salvation," there is no such thing as a purely natural man, and with this diagnosis Lee, Williams, and Harald Lindstrom all agree.

The concept of natural man, then, is man living apart from the spiritual umbilical cord, nothing linking God with man. Man in this condition is spiritually dead, separated, estranged, or asleep. In this condition there is no possibility of salvation. The question naturally arises, "Why is this man in such a condition" and "from where comes the origin of such a nature anyway?" After looking at this we shall again return to the non reality of natural man to find the key to the problem.

THE FALL OF ADAM

Wesley deals with the Fall of man very differently than most of today's scholarly attempts to describe it. He believed the garden of Eden story to be a historic reality. For him, it was not the image or picture or myth out of which we are to glean important religious truths and realities, but a real life existence.

> Such, then, was the state of man in Paradise. By the free, unmerited love of God, he was holy and happy; He knew, loved, enjoyed God, which is, in substance, life everlasting. And in this life of love, he was to continue for ever, if he continued to obey God in all things; but, if he disobeyed him in any, he was to forfeit all. "In that day," said God, "thou shalt surely die."[16]

There are four propositions we must consider for us to understand Wesley's theology in this area. First, we find that Adam was in some sense on trial for the whole of mankind. As first man Adam is the start, the original, the template for us all. Second, in Adam's fall the sentence of death was somehow wrought upon his descendents. The how's of this sentence are not always clear. Third, the new covenant, which was given to men and all mankind, was again put on a new state of personal trial. Fourth, death came to men through the new covenant.[17]

Lindstrom notes two strains of thought in Wesley's definition of sin. He finds the first to be "an inclination to evil, or a condition in which all the faculties of man—understanding and will and affections—have been

16. Wesley, *Works*, 5:54.
17. Ibid., 9:352.

perverted.[18] The second is an even stronger and more devastating definition that is even further reaching in its consequences. It becomes a "total
corruption of the whole of human nature, a corruption chiefly manifested
in atheism and idolatry, pride, self-will, and love of the world."[19]

The life in Eden was real for Wesley and from this vital and living
relationship with God, man through Adam, chose to rebel.

> Adam, in whom all mankind were then contained, freely preferred
> evil to good. He chose to do his own will, rather than the will of
> his Creator. He "was not deceived," but knowingly and deliberately
> rebelled against his Father and his King. In that moment he lost the
> moral image of God, and, in part, the natural: He commenced un-
> holy, foolish, and unhappy. And "in Adam" all died: He entitled all
> his posterity to error, guilt, sorrow, fear, pain, diseases, and death.[20]

Wesley appears here to regard sin as a knowable choice on the part
of man. This particular definition plagues some of his interpreters today,
and is really not the best definition for sin. However, at this point of our
study, to pursue the topic of sin and its good, better, or best definition, is
but to wander far afield.

He is sure that the sin of Adam reaches through all mankind, and
there are none who can escape the results of it. Even down through the
generations, all the descendents of Adam participate in its consequences.

> *As by one man*—Adam: who is mentioned, and not Eve, as being
> the representative of mankind. *Sin entered into the world*—Actual
> sin, and its consequence, a sinful nature. *And death*—With all its
> attendants. *It entered into the world*—when it entered into being;
> for till then it did not exist. *By sin*—Therefore it could not enter
> before sin. *Even so*—Namely, by one man. . . . *All sinned*—In Adam.
> These words assign the reason why death came upon *all men*: in-
> fants themselves not excepted, *in that all sinned.*[21]

The consequences of this first sin are far reaching. We have already
seen that the *moral image* of man is utterly destroyed by this sin and the
natural and *political images* suffer distortions. The whole creation of God is
deemed to have fallen from its original condition. "It is an evident truth, that

18. Lindstrom, *Wesley and Sanctification*, 27.
19. Ibid.
20. Wesley, *Works*, 6:223.
21. Wesley, *Notes*, 537.

the whole animate creation is punished for Adam's Sin."[22] Wesley speaks of all the animals of nature that have become quite different from their original creation because they too now are under the fallen condition of nature. It is the whole creation of God that has fallen, not just man.

It is important in our consideration of the Fall, for us to remember the meaning of Wesley's usage. He is not talking only about the talents, mental capacities, physical possibilities, political, or social works of man. He is thinking especially of the relation of man to God. It is in this order, the Order of Salvation, that man is fallen completely. It is in the order of salvation that man is utterly helpless, and utterly depraved: he is now man apart from God. Man may have many mental achievements and social good works, but he cannot save himself, he has not this capacity within himself. He may be capable of great things in other areas of life, but in the order of salvation he has only misery and wickedness to commend him.

> She then "gave to her husband, and he did eat." And in that day, yea, in that moment, he *died*! The life of God was extinguished in his soul. The glory departed from him. He lost the whole moral image of God,—righteousness and true holiness. He was unholy; he was unhappy; he was full of sin; full of guilt and tormenting fears.[23]

Spiritual life is utterly dependent upon God for its existence within man. At the moment of man's disobedience in Adam, the Spirit died within man. Man lost the third dimension, for there is no spiritual life apart from the source of the spiritual life—God.

Man, in deliberately disobeying God through the sin of Adam, has now entered into an existence characterized by separation from God. He who was created to live in a moment-by-moment, loving, and vital relationship with God has become separated from the source of his existence. A wedge has been driven, man is turned in upon himself, man is in rebellion, and he is utterly estranged from God. "He knows not how to get one step forward in the way. Encompassed with sin, and sorrow, and fear, and finding no way to escape, he can only cry out, 'Lord save, or I perish!'"[24]

22. Wesley, *Works*, 9:319.

23. Ibid., 6:272.

24. Wesley, *Standard Sermons*, 1:325.

Another result of the Fall is that man's nature became mortal. Before the Fall man was created to live eternally with God, but since the sin and separation, man has been mortal.[25]

> Man did disobey God. . . . His soul died, was separated from God; separate from whom the soul has no more life than the body has when separate from the soul. His body, likewise, became corruptible and mortal; so that death then took hold on this also. And being already dead in spirit, dead to God, dead in sin, he hastened on to death everlasting; to the destruction both of body and soul, in the fire never to be quenched.[26]

The death of man in the Genesis narrative is a spiritual death, which is a death of the living, intimate, relationship of a man with God. The spiritual life from God who breathed into the spirit of man is no longer alive; it is dead. It has become dead as is the body when the breath of life is removed from it.

Another strange fact brought out from a study of Wesley's interpretation of the Fall of man, is that he is sure no man will merit eternal death merely from the Fall of Adam. The sin of Adam, carried down through the generations of man, is not enough to certify the damnation of any man.

Wesley begins to answer this question by quoting Dr. John Taylor:

> "But with regard to parents and their posterity, God assures us, children 'shall not die for the iniquity of their fathers!'" No, not eternally. I believe none ever did, or ever will, die eternally, merely for the sin of our first father.[27]

This statement creates a problem for the interpreter in how to handle other quotations from Wesley that would seem to indicate the terribleness of the condition of man as a result of the Fall. Elsewhere it appears sure that the sentence of death falls upon the total of mankind for the sin of Adam.

The answer is found in his interpretation *of prevenient* or *preventing grace*. After considering the tragic situation of man—the separation, alienation, rebellion, misery, and sin that bind him—one is happy to find that Wesley makes room for prevenient grace. We find that prevenient

25. Wesley, *Works*, 6:272.
26. Wesley, *Standard Sermons*, 1:117.
27. Wesley, *Works*, 9:315.

grace lessens the terrible blow for which one otherwise would have to prepare himself.

THE PREVENIENT GRACE OF GOD

The "hairs breath" which Methodism comes in relation to Calvinism is saved by the doctrine of prevenient grace. This is the point at which Wesley differed from Calvin and his doctrine of predestination. The doctrine of original sin, coupled with that of prevenient grace, gives Methodism some of its distinctiveness.

The full sweep of Wesleyan theology will only be found when one reads a summary such as Colin S. Williams' book, *John Wesley's Theology Today*. The purpose of our thinking together does not lie in the completion of such a study. It is enough for us to consider only the beginning of the order of salvation.

> Salvation begins with what is usually termed (and very properly) *preventing grace*; including the first wish to please God, the first dawn of light concerning his will, and this first slight transient conviction of having sinned against him. All these imply some tendency toward life; some degree of salvation; the beginning of a deliverance from a blind, unfeeling heart, quite insensible of God and the things of God.[28]

We see here that Wesleyan theology is dominated by a pull towards the complete salvation, of which prevenient grace is but the first dawning step. Prevenient grace is like a spiritual magnet, continually pulling and urging man to turn towards God. For a more complete treatment of this idea, Lindstrom is helpful.[29] The point at hand is that prevenient grace is a work of God within the heart of every man. There is no man, in real life, which lives apart from this work of grace. No man is left cold, without light, wholly apart from God. God works in the heart of every man. Some receive more grace and continue to final salvation, some receive less—but the wonder is that God works in all men.

> For allowing that all the souls of men are dead in sin by *nature*, this excuses none, seeing there is no man that is in a state of mere nature; there is no man, unless he has quenched the Spirit, that is wholly void of the grace of God. No man living is entirely desti-

28. Ibid., 6:509.

29. Lindstrom, *Wesley and Sanctification*, 27.

tute of what is vulgarly called *natural conscience*. But this is not natural: It is more properly termed, *preventing grace*. Every man has a greater or less measure of this, which waiteth not for the call of man.[30]

Wesley continues, speaking of the good desires that arise in the life and mind of us all. These too are the supernatural workings of God within the life of man. He speaks of the light, even small glimmers of light, which we all have from the Light of God. This is the light sent into the world to save man.

> *Who lighteth everyman*—By what is vulgarly termed natural conscience, pointing out at least the general lives of good and evil. And this light, if man did not hinder, would shine more and more to the perfect day.[31]

He speaks of the uneasy feeling all men have when they act contrary to their conscience, which he believes to be the Light of God found in them. "So that no man sins because he has not grace, but because he does not use the grace which he hath."[32]

Even the Jew and the Heathen who are performing the Law which God has given, do so only by the prevenient grace of God. The conscience of man is the gift of God to man, for we do not naturally—as in natural man—have this conscience. Conscience is a supernatural gift, an element of prevenient grace.

All men, without exception, receive this grace as well as their salvation, through Christ. Whether man realizes it or not, it is God's grace that works within natural man for his salvation.

> *That God is not a respecter of persons*—Is not partial in His love. The words mean, in a particular sense, that He does not confine His love to one nation; in a general, that He is loving to every man, and willeth all men should be saved. . . . *Is accepted of him*—Through Christ, though he knows Him not. This assertion is express, and admits of no exception. He is in the favour of God, whether enjoying His written word and ordinances or not.[33]

---

30. Wesley, *Works*, 6:512.
31. Wesley, *Notes*, 303.
32. Wesley, *Works*, 6:512.
33. Wesley, *Notes*, 434–35.

As an element of God's prevenient grace, the conscience works freely within man. Wesley divides the office of the conscience into the three duties it performs. First, the conscience is a witness to man, telling and reminding us of what we have done. Second, the conscience acts as our judge, passing its own sentence upon the actions that we have performed. Third, the conscience executes its own sentence in some manner, giving complacency or uneasiness, depending upon the actions we have performed.[34]

Speaking of the public and moral sense contained within the conscience, Wesley declares them both supernatural gifts of God to man.

> But it is not true, that either the *public* or the *moral sense* (both of which are included in the term conscience) is now natural to man. Whatever may have been the case at first, while man was in a state of innocence, both the one and the other is now a branch of that supernatural gift of God which we usually style, preventing grace.[35]

Especially is the good conscience God's gift. It is defined as, "A divine consciousness of walking in all things according to the written word of God."[36]

Thus man is just not able to make any effort, any work at all for his salvation. Man is not the initiator of the reconciliation. Man is totally depraved in the sense that he is utterly incapable of saving himself, but even then he is not left in total depravity. Man does have the prevenient grace of God working in him, whether he will or will not accept it.

> In this world man exists as a natural man plus the prevenient grace of God. And this grace is not the forgiving favor of God granted in what the Reformed theologians called justification; this grace is empowering grace.[37]

Lindstrom and others have well pointed out that this—the doctrine of prevenient grace—is the result of a problem in the theology of John Wesley. Wesley could not allow for man's knowledge of God to arise out of our daily life, on the basis of his doctrine of original sin. In order to supply the missing link and avoid full Calvinism, he employs the doctrine of

34. Wesley, *Works*, 7:188.
35. Ibid., 7:189.
36. Ibid., 7:190.
37. Lee, *Wesley and Modern Religion*, 125.

prevenient grace. It is an effective medication, and answers many embarrassing problems, which otherwise would be extremely difficult to satisfy. Edward H. Sugden has well noted:

> He (Wesley) avoided Pelagianism by his definite teaching that through the Fall man became totally depraved, dead in trespasses and sins, without any power to resist temptation or to turn to God; but he also avoided Calvinism by his doctrine of prevenient grace, to wit, that the Holy Spirit is given to every man to reveal to him his duty and to give him power to turn to God for help and salvation [parentheses mine]. This *free gift*, he taught, comes to ALL men unto justification of life; and this true light enlightens every man that cometh into the world.[38]

Wesley steers straight between the double perils of Pelagianism[39] (there is no original sin and man has the ability within himself to choose the right path and remain sinless) and Calvinism (double predestination, man has no say in God's choice of who will be saved and who won't).

Lee finds yet other protections for Wesley. He says that Wesley effectively points out the sinful condition of man—no holds barred. He shows the utter estrangement of man living apart from God, separated and dead. At the same time, he protects the divine initiative. God can be made the single source of everything within the order of salvation. All comes to man only by the grace of God. This leaves us thankful to no one but God for all the mercies and grace given freely to us in the order of salvation.

William R. Cannon summarizes the usefulness of prevenient grace to the theology of Wesley in these words:

> . . . It means simply this: the common grace of God given unto all men alike is sufficient to bring man to see the light of the gospel truth and to lead them to repentance and to the performance of acts meet for repentance. Thus preventing grace implies some "tendency toward life; some degree of salvation; the beginning of a deliverance from a blind, unfeeling heart, quite insensible to God and the things of God." And it leads directly to "convincing grace," which is repentance.[40]

38. Wesley, *Standard Sermons*, 2:43–44.

39. Latourette, *History of Christianity*, 181.

40. Cannon, *Theology of John Wesley*, 113.

THE RESPONSIBILITY OF MAN

Something is still missing; something is still lost. If man receives the pre-venient grace of God and if no man suffers eternal death merely for the guilt of Adam's sin, why are not all men saved? If, on the other hand, all men participate in the terrible guilt Wesley portrays in his doctrine of sin, and if all men are totally corrupt and estranged from God, why are not all men condemned? The answer to this problem is found in the final link of Wesley's view of natural man as the recipient of the prevenient grace of God.

Man's *response* to God's grace is vital to a full comprehension of man. Man must respond to the prevenient grace that he receives. "Thus because God is directly at work even within the Natural Man. Therefore man is responsible; not because he is naturally free to do God's will, but because he resists God's grace."[41] Cannon points out in an excellent manner the responsibility of man in the whole order of salvation. For our purpose, he speaks of man's responsibility in regard to prevenient grace.

> Granting, therefore, man's ability to stifle and to kill the grace of God within him, have we the right to ascribe to him the positive role of a co-operator with God? We have. For in the very act of not killing grace and of listening to the voice of natural conscience, even though at times very inattentively, man is actually co-operat-ing with God in God's efforts in behalf of his salvation.[42]

This is the conclusion of a story that must be told in order to un-derstand the fullness of Wesley's theological thought. Natural man is an intellectualized description, rather than the actual condition of any man. The reason for this is revealed in our study of prevenient grace. This grace does not irresistibly turn man towards God, but allows man to choose to accept it. It offers enough light that man may make a responsible choice, one that will determine in large measure his eternal destiny.

> In other words, Wesley finds opportunity of choice on the foun-dation of grace. If, despite this privilege, man prefers to follow the inclination to evil of original sin and thus commits personal sin, he must be regarded as being himself responsible for his transgression.[43]

41. Williams, *John Wesley's Theology Today*, 42.

42. Cannon, *Theology of John Wesley*, 115.

43. Lindstrom, *Wesley and Sanctification*, 37.

Throughout the writings of Wesley on this point, he hammers home the contention that man must decide, and God has given him the power to make this decision.[44] By the grace of God, man is able to accept the grace of God or to reject God's saving grace. The condition for salvation is an acceptance of God's terms, and the grace of God has given us the power to make this choice.

> And I will have compassion on whom I will have compassion— Namely, on those only who submit to My terms, who accept of it in the way that I have appointed.[45]

Even as to the origin of sin itself, Wesley declares that it is only by the allowance and full acceptance of man. God did not want the choice to be made in this manner, but allowed man the power to so choose.

> He said, An enemy hath done this . . . God made men, as He did angels, intelligent creatures, and consequently free either to choose good or evil; but He implanted no evil in the human soul. "An enemy," with man's concurrence, "hath done this."[46]

Speaking of the call of Christ to those who would follow Him, Wesley says, "No one is forced; but if any will be a Christian, it must be on these terms."[47] Writing upon the doctrine of original sin, he hammers the point home continually—man may be separated from God, he may be a sinner, he may be alienated from the source of his life—but if he is these things, he has a choice.[48] There is abundant evidence of this idea in the hymns of Wesley also.

> Sinners, turn, why will ye die?
> God, your Maker, asks you why:
> God, who did your being give,
> Made you with himself to live;
> He the fatal cause demands,
> Asks the work of his own hands,
> Why, ye thankless creatures, why
> Will ye cross his love, and die?

44. Wesley, *Works*, 6:311.
45. Wesley, *Notes*, 557.
46. Ibid., 71.
47. Ibid., 83.
48. Wesley, *Works*, 6:498, 9:192–464.

> Dead already? Dead within,
> Spiritually dead in sin:
> Dead to God, while here you breathe,
> Pant ye after second death?
> Will you still in sin remain,
> Greedy of eternal pain?
> O ye dying sinners, why,
> Why will you for ever die?[49]

The consequence of prevenient grace being added to his doctrine of original sin is to make man's role in the order of salvation more important. This point is strongly urged again and again by Wesley.

> . . . by the grace of God we may cast away all our transgressions: Therefore, if we do not want, they are chargeable on ourselves. We *may* live; but we *will* die.[50]

In the same work, he argues closely concerning who is responsible for the sin that marks man's life. If man has no choice, it is God who must take the blame for the sin of man. But, on the other hand, if man does have something to say about it, if he does have a measure of responsibility, then it is man who must be charged for the guilt of his sin.

> In a word, God, looking on all ages, from the creation to the consummation, as a moment, and seeing at once whatever is in the hearts of all the children of men, knows every one that does or does not believe, in every age or nation. Yet what he knows, whether faith or unbelief, is in nowise caused by his knowledge. Men are as free in believing or not believing as if he did not know it all.[51]

To be sure, he argues, God gives the power whereby sin may be committed. Without God's grace in granting the breath of life, strength, intelligence, and other things necessary, man could not commit sin. Just the same, even if God is the source of man's strength to perform the sin, it is man's negligent stewardship of that strength that is the causal factor. Because of man's misuse of the powers granted him by God, man collects the tab for the guilt of the sin that has been committed.

> For it is the power of God whereby the murderer lifts up his arm, whereby the adulterer perpetrates his wickedness; full as much as

49. Wesley, *Wesley's Hymns*, no. 6, vv. 1, 4.

50. Wesley, *Works*, 9:275.

51. Ibid., 6:227.

it is his power whereby an acorn produces an oak, or a father a son. But does it follow, that God is chargeable with the sin? You know it does not follow. The power of God, vulgarly termed *nature*, acts from age to age, under its fixed rules. Yet he who this moment supplies the power by which a sinful action is committed is not chargeable with the sinfulness of that action.[52]

Most of the authors read by the writer find that Wesley does not do complete justice in accounting for the origin of sin in Adam. Likewise, he is found to be short in showing how righteous men can begat sons of iniquity, and how that which was created good in the beginning, can itself be converted into evil.

Allowing this, they push a second contention. That is, Wesley does affirm many true and helpful things, in regard to the sin of man. He does affirm sin to be the result of man's choices. This sin emerges from his desire and his own inclinations. Therefore, God is not to be blamed for the sin or the results of the sin. Lee writes:

In accordance with Catholic theology, Wesley posited a prevenient grace which enables man to accept increased grace and to go on by the help of God to higher stages of the Christian life. . . . The distinction is between man empowered to choose and man compelled to obey . . . [53]

Our study concludes that there is in real life no such actual condition of man. Natural man is the result of the Fall of Adam in the order of salvation, and utterly removed from the prevenient grace of God. In this state there is absolutely nothing man can do for his own salvation; he is totally dependent upon God. However, man is natural man plus prevenient grace.

At this very point, the prevenient grace of God enters so that man might not be absolved from his responsibilities, and God not blamed for the sin of man. God gives to each man the possibility of choice; each man lives in and by God's grace.

. . . man is the sole determinative factor in the decision of his own justification. Faith as the one condition of justification is offered unto him as a free gift by a gracious God, but then he must actively

52. Ibid., 9:335.
53. Lee, *Wesley and Modern Religion*, 126–27.

respond to that offer and reach out with the arms of true repentance to receive the gift.[54]

Man is responsible for the light God has given him. As free agents,
God has given us the power of choice, but this does not absolve us from
the consequences of our choice. We are to choose Him, and be responsible
for the degree of light God has given us.

> For he made you free agents; having an inward power of self-de-
> termination, which is essential to your nature. And he deals with
> you as free agents from first to last. As such, you may shut or open
> your eyes as you please. You have sufficient light shining all around
> you; yet you need not see it unless you will. But be assured, God is
> not well pleased with your shutting your eyes, and then saying, "I
> cannot see."[55]

---

54. Cannon, *Theology of John Wesley*, 117.
55. Wesley, *Works*, 6:311.

2

Heathenism, Indians, and Christianity

THE DEFINITION OF HEATHENISM

IN ORDER TO BEGIN to answer the problem of Heathenism's relation to Christianity we must first find out what Wesley means by the term. Terms change through the years and we find this a good example. Sugden, in his notes on *The Standard Sermons of John Wesley*, helps us understand Wesley's usage:

> Here and elsewhere Wesley uses "heathen" in the same sense of "non-Christian" . . . in the eighteenth century it had no such connotation, (uncivilized and barbarous) and is constantly used of the Greeks and Romans, without any intention of reproach or blame [parentheses mine]. So that we must beware of thinking that Wesley is sneering at Horace or Aristotle, when he speaks of them as "the heathen poet" and "the heathen moralist" respectively.[1]

The terms "Heathen," "atheism," "infidel," "dissipation," and sometimes "Indian," are not normally distinguished by Wesley. In fact, he helps us by declaring atheism and dissipation to be the same.

> From all that has been said, it may be seen, with the utmost clearness, what is the nature of that fashionable thing called dissipation. . . . It is the very quintessence of Atheism; it is artificial, added to natural, ungodliness. It is the art of forgetting God, of being altogether "without God in the world;" the art of excluding him, if not out of the world he has created, yet out of the minds of all his intelligent creatures. It is a total studied inattention to the whole invisible and eternal world; more especially to death, the gate of

---

1. Wesley, *Standard Sermons*, 1:55.

eternity, and to the important consequences of death—heaven and hell![2]

From this definition, we find the "dissipated" man in a worse condition even than natural man. This dissipated man has turned against God; he has exercised his God-given ability to choose and has actively chosen not to turn to God. Though natural man, admittedly an abstraction, has of necessity made the choice, he seems not to be as active in the process of moving apart from God as the dissipated man. All these terms are close enough, as understood by Wesley, to merit our handling them together.

Some may think that we are dealing with natural man in this section, but as we have found, there is no such man in this condition. Man is natural man plus the workings of prevenient grace that God has given to him.

In his sermon "On The Education of Children,"[3] Wesley declares that all children are by nature atheists; they are without God in the world. There is no inborn knowledge of God within us at birth; all men are atheists.[4]

> . . . it does not appear that man has naturally any more idea of God than any of the beasts of the field; he has no knowledge of God at all no fear of God at all; neither is God in all his thoughts. Whatever change may afterwards be wrought, (whether by the grace of God, or by his own reflection, or by education,) he is by nature, a mere Atheist.[5]

Wesley marvelously portrayed the condition of the atheist or the Heathen in his sermon, "On Living Without God." Here the parallel is drawn between a toad that he supposes to have lived a long time in a tree, utterly cut off from the outside world, and a Heathen.

He first states that the normal definition of the term "atheist" is inadequate. In his travels throughout the land he finds that the common meaning, of those who disbelieve in a God, has no or very little counterpart in reality. In fifty years he has found only two men who fit this common conception. Then he defines atheism as he would use it:[6]

---

2. Wesley, *Works*, 7:263–64.

3. Ibid., 7:86–98.

4. Ibid., 6:58–59.

5. Ibid., 7:89.

6. Wesley, *Works*, 6:58–59.

... such as are only practical Atheists; as have not God in all their thoughts; such as have not acquainted themselves with him, neither have any fellowship with him; such as have no more intercourse with God, or the invisible world, than this animal had with the visible.[7]

Wesley uses this person to compare with the toad in the tree. Both the toad and the atheist have all that is needed to make them a real creature, but a thick veil is drawn between them and the real world.[8] Although the Light of God is to be found, it is not perceived; although God's word has been spoken, it is not heard; although God works in his heart, it is not felt.[9] "In a word, he has no more intercourse with, or knowledge of, the spiritual world, than this poor creature had of the natural, while shut up in its dark enclosure.[10]

Wesley picks up the common term "dissipation" and gives it a religious meaning, because he feels it has been grossly misused in his day. Too often it is defined to mean merely the outward actions of the person, when in reality it ought to stand for the inner condition, which of necessity, precedes it.

We are accustomed to speak of dissipation, as having respect chiefly, if not wholly, to the outward behavior; to the manner of life. But it is within before it appears without; It is in the heart, before it is seen in the outward conversation. There must be a dissipated spirit, before there is a dissipated manner of life.[11]

He begins his argument with the statement that God has created all things for Himself. Especially is this true with regard to the intelligent beings of creation. Man has been created to know, to love, and enjoy God, and as long as man lives in this moment-by-moment relationship with God, he is spiritually healthy.

The trouble begins when we do not "attend upon" God. When we are distracted from God, who is to be the center of our attention, we turn away from Him. Our thoughts begin to wander and our daily lives distract us

7. Ibid., 7:351.
8. Ibid.
9. Ibid.
10. Ibid.
11. Ibid., 6:445.

from the purpose of our life.[12] Even the whole visible creation may draw our attention from Him within us. We are cut adrift from our mooring.

This condition is made possible because of our participation in the Fall of man. We have the tendency to wander from God, to turn from Him who is within us, from our birth.[13]

> This is the more easily done, because we are all by nature. . . .
> Atheists, in the world; and that is so high a degree, that it requires
> no less than almighty power to counteract that tendency to dis-
> sipation which is in every human spirit, and restore the capacity of
> attending to God, and fixing itself on him.[14]

Without being renewed in the image of God, a work of God's grace, it is impossible that we attend to God as we ought.

The degree to which we let ourselves become distracted from God is the degree of our dissipation. We are all atheists, Heathens, or infidels as we let ourselves be distracted from God, who is to be the center of our lives. We have no love of God, no fear of God, and we are filled with pride, self-will, and love of the world.[15] The definition of dissipation then becomes:

> He is a man that is separated from God; that is disunited from his
> centre; whether this be occasioned by hurry or business, by seek-
> ing honour or preferment, or by fondness for diversions, for silly
> pleasures, so called, or for any trifle under the sun.[16]

The Heathen is an idolater, for he gives his heart to something other than God.[17] Wesley does not trap himself by thinking only in terms of physical idols that men in ancient times have created. Idolatry for him becomes more complex and personal. It becomes the same thing as dissipation, for it is the removing of one's center from God. Idolatry is anything upon which man's center is now focused. Dissipation removes man's center from God and places it upon another center, which then becomes the idol.

Wesley lists many idols common to the Heathen. First is the "desire of the flesh," by which he means all of the outward senses. Some would

12. Ibid., 6:23–32.

13. Wesley, *Standard Sermons*, 2:182.

14. Wesley, *Works*, 6:446.

15. Ibid., 6:58–61.

16. Ibid., 6:447–48.

17. Ibid., 6:436.

seek to limit this desire to sexual pleasures and gratification, but to him it means all of the outward senses that are misused.[18]

Second is the "desire of the eye," which means the centering of the person upon happiness gained by the imagination. Beautiful objects, novelty, music, the study of languages, philosophy, and so on may become the idols of the Heathen. He hastens to tell us that these things are not bad, in and of themselves. They are bad and become idols only when the person wrongly uses them.

> I allow that most of these studies have their use, and that it is possible to *use* without *abusing* them. But if we seek our happiness in any of these things, then it commences an *idol*. And the enjoyment of it, however it may be admired and applauded by the world, is condemned by God as neither better nor worse than damnable *idolatry*.[19]

Third is the "pride of life." Usually taken to mean the splendor and pomp and circumstance of life, Wesley finds yet a deeper meaning. It means for one to seek his happiness in the praises that men may give. Persons who build reputations in order to be happy from them are building upon the sand.

Fourth is the "love of money." Many times money is used for other ends, but it may be used for its own end, and this is idolatry. An example of this would be a miser who seeks money for its own sake. "In a word, so many objects as there are in the world, wherein men seek happiness instead of seeking it in God, so many idols they set up in their hearts, so many species of idolatry they practice.[20]

Fifth is the "idolizing a human creature." After explaining that we are to love others, especially husbands and wives, Wesley contends we may still commit idolatry. We are idolaters if we love them more than we ought, if we put them in the place of God. If we give them our hearts in the manner that we ought to give them only to God, we are worshipping idols. Of course with Wesley's luck with women and wives we might not be too sure of him at this point.

Wesley is not unaware about the moral lives that some Heathens may live. He is sure many of their lives are very embarrassing to many

18. Ibid., 6:437.

19. Wesley, *Works*, 6:440.

20. Ibid., 6:441.

Christians.[21] Charles Wesley's sermon "The Almost Christian" lists three virtues that the Heathen may have. The Heathen may be honest, have some regard for truth and justice, and may be capable of offering a type of love and assistance to others.

The faith of a Heathen is far short of that found in True Christianity. The Heathen may have some conception of the divine providence of God.[22] He often believes in good and evil angels.[23] He knows God, but does not know this God of hope, as the Christian knows Him.[24] He is still under the law of God, that is, the moral precepts that God has given.[25] He is not as guilty as a Christian because he has not received the fullness of the revelation through Jesus Christ. Nevertheless, he does know God in some sense.

> *Because, knowing God*—For the wiser heathens did know that there was one supreme God; yet from low and base considerations they conformed to the idolatry of the vulgar. *They did not glorify him as God, neither were thankful*—They neither thanked Him for His benefits, nor glorified Him for His divine perfections. *But became vain*—Like the idols they worshipped. *In their reasoning's*—Various, uncertain, foolish.[26]

This, then, is the condition of the Heathen, the infidels, the dissipated, and the atheists. We will deal with Indians more specifically in the next section.

THE "NOBLE SAVAGE" FOUND AND LOST

The founder of Methodism completely changed his views concerning the Indians. He started with much the same opinion as those exponents of the "noble savage." However, one must say that when he had contact with them, he certainly changed his mind.

It is hardly conceivable that one could have a higher opinion about the Heathen of America than Wesley did before he went to America and came into contact with them. His praise hardly knows bounds as he describes their condition. In 1735 he writes to Dr. John Burton:

21. Ibid., 7:201.
22. Ibid., 6:313.
23. Ibid., 6:361.
24. Wesley, *Notes*, 577.
25. Ibid., 612.
26. Ibid., 521.

They have no comments to construe away the text, no vain philosophy to corrupt it, no luxurious, sensual, covetous, ambitious exposures to soften its unpleasing truths, to reconcile earthly-mindedness and faith, the Spirit of Christ and the spirit of the world. They have no duty, no interest to serve, and are therefore fit to receive the gospel in its simplicity. They are as little children, humble, willing to learn, and eager to do the will of God, and consequently they shall know of every doctrine I preach whether it be of God. By these therefore I hope to learn the purity of that faith which was once delivered to the saints; the genuine sense and full extent of those laws which none can understand who mind earthly things.[27]

He grants to the Heathens the best in human nature, which he later takes away in his understanding of the doctrine of Original Sin.[28]

One finds trouble accepting Wesley's credulity in believing these things about the condition of the Indian in America. However, if we realize that when he wrote the above he had no contact with the Indians, and his information came from a limited knowledge of the English people concerning them, it becomes more understandable. For example, his report of them in the *Standard Sermons*, XXIII, point 9.

Sugden's comment is pertinent at this point.

Evidently Wesley, like many of his contemporaries, was still suffering from the illusion that the Indians were living the simple life of nature, free from all the vices of European civilization. "The Noble Red Man" was idealized into something very different from the fact.[29]

On the eve of his departure to America, Wesley was going forth to spread the gospel of Jesus Christ among the natives of America, the Indians. They were waiting in eagerness to receive, and able to clarify and correct him if he made mistakes in presenting the gospel, because they were free and pure from the vices of his culture.

A more remarkable mixture of learning and ignorance, of piety and pretension, of dogmatism and devotion, than that which made up the character of John Wesley at this transitional period of his life, is difficult to imagine.... Civilization has its vices, which interfere with his great desire for holiness; he therefore eagerly exchanges it for barbarism, and dreams of saving his soul with the help of an Indian hut.[30]

27. Wesley, *Journal*, 8:288–89.

28. Wesley, *Works*, 9:192–464.

29. Wesley, *Standard Sermons*, 1:479.

30. Daniels, *Illustrated History of Methodism*, 107–8.

To be sure, Wesley was not alone in his mistaken view of the Indians. This was common within the whole enlightenment world. Wesley soon gave up the idea that the Indians in their primitive purity missed the corruptions of civilization.[31]

His first meeting with the Indians was unusual, because he met those who had been acquainted with Christianity. He was not met by others, who had no knowledge of Christianity, but with those who agreed with the words of Tomochachi: "I will go up and speak to the wise men of our nation; and I hope they will hear . . . we would be taught before we are baptized."[32] Some of these notions of Wesley had a hard time dying.

Most of his knowledge came from the Indian traders and we therefore should not take all that he says about the Indians at face value.[33] The traders had nothing to lose in painting the Indians in the worst possible light.[34] In fact it made their use of force and graft against the Indians more acceptable to others.

Another consequence of Wesley's experiences with the "Heathen of America" is that he found the Indians impure in their knowledge of God.[35] It was not as easy to teach the Indians as he had imagined.

> Like so many other evangelistic leaders, Wesley had to learn that in
> the proclamation of truth an understanding of the mind receiving
> the truth is quite as important as the mind of the one uttering it.[36]

Francis J. McConnell ascribes Wesley's apparent lack of interest in backward people of the world after this time to this well learned lesson.[37]

Wesley is not nearly as gracious in his summary of the American Indian after some actual experiences with them, as we have said.[38] He gives opinions of the Indians of Georgia, as well as the Choctaw, Cherokee, Uchee, and Creek Indians, in a December 2, 1737 extract.[39] "Gone was Wesley's view of the noble savage, innocent in his simplicity and eager to

31. Wesley, *Journal*, 1:368.

32. Ibid., 1:160.

33. Wesley, *Standard Sermons*, 2:110; *Journal*, 1:396.

34. Wesley, *Journal*, 1:252.

35. Ibid., 1:367–68.

36. McConnell, *John Wesley*, 47.

37. Ibid., 48.

38. Wesley, *Journal*, 1:367–68.

39. Ibid., 1:406–9.

receive the gospel truth. He now saw human nature in a different light— mean, selfish, sinful; ignorant of God, and indifferent to saving truth."[40]

Indeed, he learned that the Indian was a savage after all and not the "noble savage" as he had thought.[41] Also, he learned that many of the white men were not noble either but were savages themselves. This fortified his belief in the doctrine of the Depravity of Man.

> Now he met men face to face in situations which gave full vent to their passions and evil will. His belief in natural depravity received no setback here; it is likely that he saw more clearly than ever that Christian Perfection is an ideal not to be obtained but by the grace of God.[42]

In the doctrine of original sin Wesley takes up the situation of the Indians in America. He spares nothing in telling of their awful condition. We must remember again that he is speaking not fully from his direct experiences with Indians, but quite a bit through experiences and talk of the traders and trappers of the American frontier.

After giving a run-down of the many Heathens throughout the world, he starts on the American Indian. As far as religious condition is concerned, he finds a difference between the northern and the southern Indians.

> Those in the north are idolaters of the lowest kind. If they do not worship the devil appearing in person, (which many firmly believe they do, many think incredible), certainly they worship the most vile and contemptible idols . . . their idols are more horrid and deformed than anything in the visible creation; and their whole worship is at once the highest affront to the divine, and disgrace to the human, nature.[43]

To the Indians of the south, Wesley ascribes no religion at all.[44] Through all his experiences and study in America, Wesley is not aware of any worship at all of these Indians.

McConnell believes that Wesley is unfair in his later description of the Indians, but thinks that even then it is more true to life than that of

---

40. Cannon, *Theology of John Wesley*, 72–73.

41. Wesley, *Journal*, 1:367–68.

42. Lee, *Wesley and Modern Religion*, 72–73.

43. Wesley, *Works*, 9:211.

44. Ibid., 9:212.

John-Jacques Rousseau,[45] for Wesley's work did stop some of the fanciful thinking of the English concerning the Indians.

HEATHENS AND SALVATION

Now we turn to the prospects of salvation for the Heathen. The Christian is faced with a multitude of problems when dealing with such a person as this. Indeed, one is hesitant to make any answer at all concerning the problem. Wesley does plead ignorance for the Christian at this point. The man, who had the world as his parish, had so because God wills that all men be saved. If God did not wish all to be saved, Wesley's parish would have to be considerably smaller. Through Christ, God has made a ransom for the whole world.

> Lord over all, if thou hast made,
>   Hast ransom'd, every soul of man,—
> Why is the grace so long delay'd?
>   Why unfulfilled the saving plan?
> The bliss for Adam's race design'd,
> When will it reach to all mankind?
>
> As lightening launch'd from east to west,
>   The coming of thy kingdom be;
> To thee, by angel-hosts confest,
>   Bow every soul and every knee;
> Thy glory let all flesh behold!
> And then fill up thy heavenly fold.[46]

He contends that the work of Christ is for the world and not for just a few here and there, who may believe and follow the Father's will. The work of Christ is for all, not just for the few.

> *Is acceptable in the sight of God our Saviour*—Who has actually saved us that believe, and *willeth all men to be saved.* It is strange that any whom He has actually saved should doubt the universality of His grace![47]

---

45. McConnell, *John Wesley*, 47.
46. Wesley, *Wesley's Hymns*, no. 444, vv. 1, 4.
47. Wesley, *Notes*, 774.

The work of Christ is "for every man that ever was or will be born into the world."[48] This message is upon the lips of Christ in His prayer to the Father.[49] The Father sent the Son for all nations,[50] for all men.[51] Through the work of the Son, the Father is seeking to reconcile the world.[52] The Father has promised the world to Christ.[53]

Since God has worked through the Son for the whole world, and since all men have not received the grace offered, it is the response of man that has made the difference. At all stages of the order of salvation, God has given to man the possibility of choice. Grace is given that men become capable of making the decision, and making it responsibly.

The bulk of mankind has no fellowship with God at all.[54] They have not been left in the dark completely, but have been given a choice. Wesley begins by quoting Dr. Taylor:

> "Again: He affirms, the Gentiles had light sufficient to have seen God's eternal power and Godhead" (Rom 1:19–21). They had; but how does it appear that this was the merely natural light of their own unassisted reason? If they had assistance from God, and did not use it, they were equally without excuse.[55]

The atheist is without excuse for not believing, for at all times and in all ages, God has been revealing Himself. There is no age in which He has been without a witness. "*He left not himself without witness*—For the heathens had always from God Himself a testimony both of His existence and of His providence."[56] The power and Godhead of God has been revealed in all ages and all may find these in the world. Even in this fallen world it is possible for man to see evidence of God.

> "His eternal power and Godhead," the existence of a powerful and eternal Being, may still be inferred from these his works, grand

---

48. Ibid., 815.

49. Ibid., 376.

50. Ibid., 317.

51. Wesley, *Notes*, 749, 774.

52. Ibid., 657.

53. Ibid., *Notes,* 534.

54. Wesley, *Works*, 9:283.

55. Ibid., 9:268.

56. Wesley, *Notes*, 450.

and magnificent, though in ruin. Consequently, these leave the Atheist without excuse.[57]

In a form of conclusion from this line of argument, Wesley states we dare not say that none of the Heathen will be saved. Though the gods of the Heathen be devils,[58] though they do not know the important doctrines of the Son and the Holy Spirit,[59] though they do not know the God of hope,[60] still, we dare not say that such a person is excluded. This person may have a weak form of faith.[61]

Most of mankind has no intimate relationship with God, no fellowship with Him.[62] Yet, we dare not draw the line: "I dare not carry them so far as to say, no Heathen shall be saved."[63] The Christian, then, cannot exclude others from salvation; we must leave it to God.[64]

Some Heathen will be saved, in large measure due to their sincerity.[65] God will reward sincerity if it is true and is continued. God will count this form of sincerity as true faith.

> But this we know, that he is not the God of the Christians only, but the God of the Heathens also; that he is "rich in mercy to all that call upon him," according to the light they have; and that "in every nation, he that feareth God and worketh righteousness is accepted of him."[66]

God will save the Heathen, but it will be by His grace, for it still is necessary that they believe and observe the laws of God.[67] These are the workings of God's grace within the heart, which He performs for the Heathen's salvation.[68]

---

57. Wesley, *Works*, 9:322.
58. Wesley, *Journal*, 1:366–67.
59. Wesley, *Works*, 6:506–7.
60. Wesley, *Notes*, 577.
61. Wesley, *Works*, 6:355–57.
62. Ibid., 9:283.
63. Ibid., 9:323.
64. Ibid., 7:48.
65. Ibid., 8:288.
66. Ibid., 7:48
67. Wesley, *Notes*, 434–35.
68. Ibid., 525.

The Heathen must pursue the object of his belief with sincerity and fulfill within his life the commandments of God.[69]

> Now, God requireth of a Heathen to believe, "that God is; that he is a rewarder of them that diligently seek him;" and that he is to be sought by glorifying him as God, by giving him thanks for all things, and by a careful practice of moral virtue, of justice, mercy, and truth, toward their fellow creatures.[70]

All of these mercies of God are worked through Christ. The whole world has been promised to Christ.[71] He is for all men; the Father sent the Son for all nations.[72] All who come to God come through the mediation of Christ, in the one fold, whether they know it or not.

> *That in the dispensation of the fullness of the times*—In this last administration of God's fullest grace, which took place when the time appointed was fully come. *He might gather together into one in Christ*—Might recapitulate, reunite, and place in order again under Christ, their common Head. *All things which are in heaven, and on earth*—All angels and men, whether living or dead, in the Lord.[73]

All those who are received by God come through Christ, for Christ is in all who are thus renewed.[74]

Wesley does allow ignorance to work in the favor of the Heathen. He thinks that all must accept the Trinity, who are to have vital religion. However, he does leave the opening for ignorance in the case of the "honest Heathen."

> Therefore, I do not see how it is possible for any to have vital religion who denies that these Three are One. And all my hope for them is, not that they will be saved during their unbelief, (unless on the footing of honest Heathens, upon the plea of invincible ignorance), but that God, before they go hence, will "bring them to the knowledge of the truth."[75]

---

69. Wesley, *Works*, 8:337; *Notes*, 432.
70. Wesley, *Works*, 5:8.
71. Wesley, *Notes*, 534.
72. Ibid., 749.
73. Ibid., 703.
74. Ibid., 749.
75. Wesley, *Works*, 6:206.

Thereby, we see that Wesley does think some Heathen will be saved. This salvation is purely by the grace of God; however man does have the choice and responsibility. Though the Heathen is not aware of Christ as the basis of his salvation, in reality, such is the case, for God is seeking to bring all together with Christ as the common Head. He is sure of the extreme difficulty for the Heathen to be saved. Wesley does not think that very many will be saved, but feels safest in leaving the matter to God, and commending Christ to his own listeners.[76]

A case in point is Wesley's *Journal*, in which he notes after the reading of the *Meditations of Marcus Antonius*:

> I make no doubt but that this is one of those "many" who "shall come from the east and the west, and sit down with Abraham, Isaac, and Jacob," while "the children of the kingdom," nominal Christians, are "shut out."[77]

HEATHENISM AND CHRISTIANITY

Wesley was not guilty of making Heathenism and Christianity equal in any sense. Rather he finds them to be poles apart.[78] In two sermons Wesley discusses the various dispensations of God to the peoples of the world.

The first sermon, "On Divine Providence," discusses the providence of God in relation to all of mankind, all Christians, and the real Christians. Three concentric circles are used to describe these three providences. The outermost circle stands for God's love for all mankind.

> His love is not confined: "The Lord is loving unto every man, and his mercy is over all his works." He careth for the very outcasts of men: It may truly be said,
> Free as the air thy bounty streams
> O'er all thy works: Thy mercies' beams
> Diffusive as thy sun's arise.[79]

In the second sermon, "On Faith," Wesley discusses eight types of faith. They are: Materialist, Deist, Heathen, Jew, John the Baptist, Roman Catholic, Protestant, and saving faith. Heathens have a very immature and

76. Ibid., 6:348, 7:48.
77. Wesley, *Journal*, 3:215.
78. Wesley, *Works*, 6:63.
79. Ibid., 6:319.

inadequate faith but they are not to be blamed so much as to be pitied for the narrowness of their faith. "And their not believing the whole truth, it is not due to want of sincerity, but merely to want of light."[80] These two sermons help show us that Wesley makes a great distinction between Christianity and Heathenism.

The problem with the Heathen is that he, like many others, has sought the externals of religion rather than the inner religion of the heart.[81] The Heathen makes the outer show of religion, but has not the inner reality. He has sought to remove God from religion and make a religion out of humanity.

The Heathens do have some great truths, but they are ignorant of the two grand doctrines of the Christian faith. These two are the doctrines of Christ as the Son of God (Incarnation) and the Holy Spirit.[82] They have some knowledge of the invisible world,[83] but the natural manners of men are not enough to fill in all the gaps and enable them to find a good religion, much less Christianity.[84]

The Heathen is to change or convert to Christianity. This is the impetus of the Christian mission and Christian preaching. This change comes about through the activity of the Holy Spirit. "To change one of these heathens into a real Christian, and to continue him such, all the ordinary operations of the Holy Spirit are absolutely necessary."[85]

Wesley is sure that mankind needs Christianity. Even the Heathen have full need of Him as priest, prophet, and king.

> We are by nature at a distance from God, alienated from Him, and incapable of a free access to Him. Hence we want a Mediator, an Intercessor; in a word, a Christ in His priestly office. This regards our state with respect to God. And with respect to ourselves, we find a total darkness, blindness, ignorance of God, and the things of God. Now here we want Christ in His prophetic office, to enlighten our minds, and teach us the whole will of God. We find also within us a strange misrule of appetites and passions. For these

---

80. Ibid., 7:197.

81. Ibid., 8:19–20.

82. Ibid., 6:506.

83. Ibid., 7:258–59.

84. Ibid., 9:148.

85. Wesley, *Letters,* 4:376.

we want Christ in His royal character, to reign in our hearts, and subdue all things to Himself.[86]

Man has full need of all that Christ has done and performed for him. We have to be in Christ to share in the Kingdom.[87] We have to repent of our sin, which is a universal demand.[88] Christianity begins where Heathenism leaves off.[89]

The saving faith of a Christian is a far cry from the dim light of the Heathen. The Christian knows Christ and is convinced of the works that God has done through Him. This faith is the gift of God to the one who seeks and therefore finds. If he endures to the end, he shall find salvation and eternal life.

> It (faith) is, according to St. Paul, an . . . "evidence" or "conviction" (which is totally different from a desire) "of things not seen" a supernatural, a divine evidence and conviction of the things which God hath revealed in His Word: of this in particular, that the Son of God hath loved me and given Himself for me [parentheses mine]. Whosoever hath this faith is born. Whosoever thus believeth is saved; and if he endure therein to the end, shall be saved everlastingly.[90]

Wesley holds the doctrine of original sin as a separating factor. He is sure that the Heathen misunderstands and does not find the full significance of the doctrine, as a Christian does. Thus, the doctrine of original sin becomes one of Christianity's chief bulwarks against Heathenism.

Wesley, in writing to Dr. Taylor concerning Taylor's interpretation of the doctrine of original sin, thinks that their differences are extreme. In the difference between their interpretation of this one doctrine, Wesley finds the differences between Christianity and Heathenism.[91]

> It is Christianity or heathenism! For, take away the scriptural doctrines of Redemption or Justification, and that of the New Birth, the beginning of sanctification, or (which amounts to the same) explain them as you do, suitably to your doctrine of Original Sin,

86. Wesley, *Notes*, 16.
87. Ibid., 361.
88. Ibid., 466.
89. Wesley, *Works*, 5:256.
90. Wesley, *Letters*, 3:359.
91. Wesley, *Works*, 6:63.

and what is Christianity better than heathenism? Wherein, save in rectifying some of our notions, has the religion of St. Paul any pre-eminence over that of Socrates or Epictetus?[92]

The healing of Heathenism lies in the Heathen turning to the God known in Christ. God, by His mercy, heals us of our sickness, of our Heathenism, by the knowledge of Jesus Christ. He gives to us the gift of faith in His son, which is the cure of our disease.

> God heals all our Atheism by the knowledge of Himself, and of Jesus Christ whom he hath sent; by giving us faith, a divine evidence and conviction of God, and of the things of God—in particular, of this important truth, "Christ loved *me*, and gave himself for *me*.[93]

As the final blow, the final word upon the relation of Heathenism to Christianity, Wesley speaks of the unity of mankind, and the unity of God. There is but one God who is Lord and Father over all. This God has sustained the whole creation, and even us, to the present moment. Because of the one God there is one religion and a single happiness for all men. Christianity is the one religion for the whole world, since God has worked the salvation of the whole world through Christ.

In his sermon "The Unity of the Divine Being," Wesley makes this point over and over. He drives home the perfection, eternity, omnipresence, omnipotence, omniscience, holiness, and spiritual nature of the one God. The Christian knows of the oneness of humanity, oneness of God, and therefore the oneness of religion for the total of mankind.[94]

> And as there is one God, so there is one religion and one happiness for all men. God never intended there should be any more; and it is not possible there should. Indeed, in another sense, as the Apostle observes, "there are gods many, and lords many." All the heathen nations had their gods; and many, whole shoals of them. And generally, the more polished they were, the more gods they heaped up to themselves. But to us, to all that are favored with the Christian Revelation, "There is but one God;" who declares of himself, "Is there any God beside me? There is none; I know not any."[95]

92. Wesley, *Letters*, 4:67.
93. Wesley, *Works*, 6:64.
94. Ibid., 7:271.
95. Ibid., 7:264.

John and Charles Wesley long for the day in which all people of God shall meet in peace and unity. They seek the outpouring of God's grace, which will bring the people in from east, west, north, and south. One great fellowship under the Father of Jesus Christ, is the goal of all mankind, Heathen as well as Christian.

> Happy day of union sweet!
>   O when shall it appear!
> When shall all thy people meet
>   In amity sincere!
> Tear each other's flesh no more,
> But kindly think and speak the same;
>   All express the meekening power
>   And spirit of the Lamb!
> Visit us, bright Morning Star,
>   And bring the perfect day!
> Urged by faith's incessant prayer,
>   No longer, Lord delay:
> Now destroy the envious root;
> The ground of nature's feuds remove;
>   Fill the earth with golden fruit,
>   With ripe, millennial love.[96]

And, how shall the True Christian act towards his Heathen brother? Though some would belittle them, and say we need not keep faith with them, others have no dealings with them. Wesley says we are to treat them with mercy, as the neighbor we are commanded to love. "And the more they are filled with the life of God, the more tenderly will they be concerned for those who are still without God in the world, still dead in trespasses and sins."[97] Rather than hate them, Christians are "those who, far from despising, earnestly grieve for, those that do not hunger after God."[98]

A full discussion of this relationship between the True Christian and those lost in their sins is found in part III of Wesley's sermon, "Upon Our Lord's Sermon Upon the Mount: II."[99]

---

96. Wesley, *Wesley's Hymns*, no. 449.
97. Wesley, *Standard Sermons*, 1:345.
98. Ibid., 1:346.
99. Ibid., 1:345–54.

3

Judaism and Christianity

THE TRUE JEW

IN DEALING WITH THE Jewish dispensation, Wesley appears to be on
more slippery ground than he is in dealing with most of the others.
Part of the reason seems to lie in the very great closeness of Judaism
to Christianity. Judaism is the soil from which Christianity grew. The
Christian Lord and Savior was Himself a Jew. The apostles were Jews in
the beginning, and some of them took a long time before realizing the
differences between their Jewish heritage and the new life in Christ. So
close is the relationship between the two, that the Wesleyan hymnbook
has this hymn:

> Father of faithful Abraham, hear
>> Our earnest suit for Abraham's seed!
> Justly they claim the softest prayer
>   From us, adopted in their stead,
> Who mercy through their fall obtain,
> And Christ by their rejection gain.[1]

Wesley speaks of the Jew who lived before Christ and the Jew who lived
after Christ. The Jew before Christ is easier to be dealt with. The Jew before Christ was living under the former dispensation of God and had the
light that was then given to man. His faith centered on the Scripture that
was then written and belief in the Messiah who was to come and bring
newness of life.

---

1. Wesley, *Wesley's Hymns*, no. 451, v. 1.

> By Jewish faith, I mean, the faith of those who lived between the giving of the law and the coming of Christ. These, that is those that were serious and sincere among them, believed all that is written in the Old Testament. In particular, they believed that, in the fullness of time, the Messiah would appear, "to finish the transgression, to make an end of sin, and bring in everlasting righteousness."[2]

The Jew who lived after Christ is harder for Wesley to handle theologically because the new work through Christ has been performed, and a new covenant has been given to mankind.[3]

The true Jew is one of God's people, and therefore not just one having the outer show of religion. Religion, to Wesley, is always an inner relationship of the person with God, not the outer performance of the requirements that God may make. The outer requirements are important to Wesley—witness his emphasis upon the saraments—but the inner relationship is primary. The true Jew had this inner relationship, in the inner soul, a saving relationship with God.

This relationship, as in Christianity, was productive of the fruit of righteousness. It brought inner parity and renewal by the Spirit of God within the person. God is found and contacts us within the inner recesses of the heart, and by this reality a true Jew may be known.

> *For he is not a Jew*—In the most important sense, that is, one of God's beloved people. *Who is one in outward show only*; *Neither is that* the true, acceptable *circumcision, which is apparent in the flesh.*
>
> *But he is a Jew*—That is, one of God's people. *Who is one inwardly*—In the secret recesses of his soul. And the acceptable *circumcision is that of the heart*—referring to Deuteronomy 30:6; the putting away all inward impurity. This is seated *in the spirit,* the inmost soul, renewed by the Spirit of God. *And not in the letter*—Not in the external ceremony. *Whose praise is not from men, but from God*—The only searcher of the heart.[4]

The true Jew is not the one who had physically been circumcised. The religious reality of circumcision is much more meaningful than this. The heart must be circumcised as well as the body. The circumcision ac-

2. Wesley, *Works*, 7:197.

3. Ibid., 8:287.

4. Wesley, *Notes*, 527.

ceptable to God is an internal circumcision. This circumcision puts away all unrighteousness, and leads to the performance of righteousness.

This inward nature of the Jew is to be found in his obedience to the laws that God has given. The Jew, by obeying the laws of God, is a servant of God. His obedience is rendered to God out of fear for Him. This is the faith of a servant, which is one of the lower forms of faith.

> Q. Who is a Jew, inwardly?

> A. A servant of God: One who sincerely obeys him out of fear.[5]

Even though they obeyed out of fear, they were made clean by this faith. Though this is a lower form of faith than others, it is an acceptable one through the Jewish dispensation.

The Jewish faith is a faith without the Holy Spirit, for the fullness of the Spirit came only after Christ.

> Q. By what faith were the Apostles clean before Christ died?

> A. By such a faith as this; by a Jewish faith: For "the Holy Ghost was not then given."[6]

Participants of the "Minutes" conversation of Tuesday, May 13, 1746, discussed this faith previously. The conversation is found in the *Works* and is described by Jonathan Reeves as:

> I had first a strong hope that God would deliver me: And this brought a degree of peace. But I had not that solid peace of God till Christ was revealed to me.[7]

This is the Jewish faith about which Wesley is speaking. This Jewish faith is found in those who were just beginning in Christ, those who grew further until they received the faith in Christ.

Again, the Jewish faith is described as residing in a person who fears God, seeks to obey Him, and yet who walks in much darkness. This believer does not have the Light of Christ, which Wesley believes to be the final and unique revelation of God to man.

5. Wesley, *Works*, 8:287–88.

6. Wesley, *Works*, 8:287.

7. Ibid.

> Q. Of whom then do you understand these words,—"Who is among you that feareth the Lord, that obeyed the voice of his servant, that walketh in darkness, and hath no light? (Isa 1:10)."

> A. Of a believer under the Jewish dispensation; one in whose heart God hath not yet shined, to give him the light of the glorious love of God in the face of Jesus Christ.[8]

The true Jew, then, is one who is born and lives under the dispensation before Christ. He has not the Light of God, which has come through the Son of God. He is inwardly renewed and finds fellowship with God by the circumcision of the heart. However, his obedience to the laws of God is on the level of the servant, rather than the Son of God.

THE JEWISH DISPENSATION

The Jewish dispensation is quite different from the Christian. The Jew of necessity has far less light than does the Christian. Though Wesley at times maintains that the Jew has not *the* light, he does think some light is given to them. Even this small and dim light that the Jew has is much more than the light enjoyed by the Heathens.

In fact, the Jews were those who first were entrusted with the oracles of God. God called them into a special relationship, a relationship in which the Light of God was given to them to be shed abroad. Because of this relationship with God, they had an amazing amount of knowledge concerning God, man, and the relationship existing between God and man. It is even through the Jews that the Messiah was to come into the world. In summarizing Rev. John Fletcher's works Wesley writes:

> But a far more considerable degree of light was vouchsafed to the Jewish nation; inasmuch as to them "were entrusted" the grand means of light, "the oracles of God." Hence many of these had clear and exalted views of the nature and attributes of God; of their duty to God and man; yes, and of the great promise made to their posterity, that "the seed of the woman should bruise the serpent's head."[9]

The Jews had sacraments used for Heathens after their conversion to Judaism. Those sacraments Wesley declares to be valid. When the Heathen

8. Ibid.
9. Ibid., 7:195.

believed that Judaism was the religion of God, and sought entrance into the community of faith, he was baptized. This sacrament was given even before circumcision.

By virtue of this baptism, it was believed he was born again, made into a new man. He was turned from a "child of the devil" to a "child of God." This engrafting of the Heathen into the vine of Judaism was considered to be a new birth.

Wesley discusses these ideas in his sermon, "The New Birth."[10] He traces the soil out of which the Christian doctrine of the New Birth had sprung and was nourished. He wonders that Nicodemus seemed to know so little about this type of new birth when Jesus was speaking to him, and declares that man may not be physically reborn, but spiritually it is possible with God.

> They cannot be literally:—A man cannot "enter a second time into his mother's womb, and be born:"—But they may spiritually: A man may be born from above, born of God, born of the Spirit, in a manner which bears a very near analogy to the natural birth.[11]

He believes these sacraments to convey saving grace to those who hear and respond to them. In speaking of the clergy and their administration of the sacraments and their ability to convey the means of grace, he declares with the ancient fathers of the Church, that the purity of the minister is not a necessity for the grace of God to work.

The priest may indeed be a sinner, but the saving grace of God may still work through his administrations and save those who receive.

> . . . Did the Jewish sacraments convey no saving grace to the hearers, because they were administered by unholy men? If so, none of the Israelites were saved from the time of Eli to the coming of Christ. . . . But who still dare to affirm this? Which is no less, in effect than to affirm, that all the children of Israel went to hell for eleven or twelve hundred years together![12]

Again, notice that Wesley is here speaking of the Jews before the new dispensation made available through Christ. The ancient Jew is the one that he is calling to our attention, not the modern counterpart.

---

10. Wesley, *Standard Sermons*, 2:226–43.

11. Wesley, *Works*, 6:69.

12. Ibid., 8:183.

The Jew is to adhere to the ritual law.[13] Though Wesley often thought of this as a bondage to the law, or as the obedience rendered by a servant rather than a son, he is mindful of the good qualities of individual Jews. An entry of the *Journal* for April 4, 1737 reads:

> I began learning Spanish, in order to converse with my Jewish parishioners; some of whom seem nearer to the mind that was in Christ than many of those who call Him Lord.[14]

This is quite an admission for one who so strongly believed in Christ and the salvation made available for the whole of mankind, which is to be found in Him. Of course, one may argue that Wesley refers only to their ethics, but this does not seem to be the correct interpretation to me. Wesley speaks of "the mind that was in Christ," and this means definitely more than just an ethic.

In line with his division of the Jews into the ancient and the modern, is his belief that the Jewish dispensation stopped with the death of Christ. The moment of Christ's death brought in the new dispensation and the old ceased, "for as the Jewish dispensation ceased at the death of Christ, consequently so did the authority of its rulers."[15]

The dispensation God worked through His prophet Moses was a great work. Through this dispensation the Jewish church was instituted, the prophecy given which led to the deliverance of the Jews from the Egyptians, and the word of God was received by them through God's spokesman Moses.

THE JEWISH FAILURE

The Jews failed to leave the old dispensation and enter the new. They were guilty of a great darkness, as much as were the Heathens. In reality they were more guilty. They walked by themselves, and not with the God of their fathers. They were alienated from God, separated from Him who was the source of their creation and the one who continued His work of sustenance.

> . . . the Jews having been just as wicked before their conversion as the Heathens. Both the one and the other had "walked," till then, "in the vanity of their mind; having their understanding darkened,"

13. Wesley, *Letters*, 8:268.
14. Wesley, *Journal*, 1:345–46.
15. Wesley, *Notes*, 404.

being equally "dead in trespasses and sins," equally "alienated from the life of God, through the blindness of their heart:"[16]

Wesley, always interested in inner religion, the religion of the heart, as opposed to a formal religion of performance, speaks against one common error of the Jews. The Jews were too often expressing their religion totally in the performance of certain ritual or ceremonial requirements of the law.

The Jew was insisting in making his religion a religion of meat and drink,[17] and not of the Kingdom—not out of righteousness, or peace, or joy.

> It is well known, that not only the unconverted Jews, but great numbers of those who had received the faith of Christ, were, notwithstanding, "zealous of the law" (Acts 21:20), even the ceremonial law of Moses. Whatsoever, therefore, they found written therein, either concerning meat and drink offerings, of the distinction between clean and unclean meats, they not only observed themselves, but vehemently pressed the same even on those "among the gentiles" (or Heathens) "who were turned to God;" yea, to such a degree, that some of them taught whosoever they came among them, "Except ye be circumcised, and keep the law," (the whole ritual law), "ye cannot be saved."[18]

This passage is found just prior to Wesley's declaration that true religion, both Judaism and Christianity, is not of the outer performance but a matter of the heart. Man must be turned to God, and this relationship will usher forth in righteousness, peace, and joy.

Wesley declares that from their light, which God has graciously given them in the Jewish dispensation, the Jews ought to know three things. First, they ought to be "taught of God," for He is the one who gives understanding to man. This understanding he does not find among the modern Jew.

> Are you taught of God? Hath he opened your understanding? Have you the inward knowledge of the Most High? I fear not. Perhaps you know little more, even of the meaning of the words, than a Mahometan.[19]

---

16. Wesley, *Works*, 9:266.

17. Ibid., 5:77.

18. Ibid.

19. Ibid., 8:191.

Second, the Jew ought to know that the essence of the Scripture is relating oneself to God by loving Him with heart, soul, and strength. Likewise, he ought to love his neighbor as he loves himself. Again, he does not find that the Jews are living up to the light that they have received. The knowledge of this lack leads Wesley to probe into the inner recesses of the heart to find out why the Jews are not living up to the light they have received.

> Why then you do not love God at all, though you will sometimes condescend to use him. You love the world. This possesses your heart. This, therefore, is your god. You renounce the God of your fathers, the God of Israel; you are still uncircumcised in heart. Your own conscience bears witness, you in this no more hear Moses and the prophets, than you do Jesus of Nazareth.[20]

Third, Wesley points out that the Jew ought to know that if he is loving God and his neighbor as he should, his fruit would bear testimony to this fact. The fruit of this love is obedience to God, and a life of righteousness and purity. The Jew of today has not reformed himself from the sins of his fathers, but walks in the same disobedient paths. Wesley calls upon them to repent of their ways:

> O Lord, we have sinned, we have rebelled against thee, neither have we obeyed the voice of the Lord our God. Yet, O our God, incline thine ear, and hear: open thine eyes, and behold our desolations; for we do not present our supplications before thee for our righteousness, but for thy great mercies.[21]

Further failures of the Jews are found discussed in the *Notes*. The Jews have robbed God in that they have taken away the glory that is due to Him alone. Wesley backs these charges against the ancient Jew by saying:

> None of these charges were rashly advanced against the Jews of that age; for, as their own historian related, some even of the priests lived by rapine, and others in gross uncleanness. And as for sacrilegiously robbing God and His altar, it had been complained of ever since Malachi: so that the instances are given with great propriety and judgment.[22]

---

20. Ibid., 8:191–92.

21. Ibid., 8:192.

22. Wesley, *Notes*, 526.

The Jews transgress against their own law,[23] and are about to be shut out of the Kingdom of God.[24] For the ingathering of the Gentiles, the Jews have no reason to murmur because it is of their own doing.[25] The Jews who reject the gospel in Christ are of first rank as criminals,[26] and some of them first called will be rejected and not enter into the Kingdom.[27]

The Jew as well as the Gentile is to become a proselyte to Christ.[28] This is the proper course for all men. The Jews who reject Christ will find themselves no different in their situation than the Heathens,[29] but those who receive Him will become sons of God.[30]

Wesley finds various failures of the Jews, past as well as present, which he reports in his assorted writings. Through it all runs his belief that they are not fulfilling the requirements they received in the dispensation into which they have been called. They are not fulfilling in their life the light that has been given to them. More basic than all this for Wesley is the fact, or expression of the fact, that the religion into which they have come has remained an external performance, rather than a vital, living, inner, dynamic relationship with God. The heart has remained uncircumcised; therefore the circumcision of the flesh is of no avail. In words sounding extremely harsh to the ear, Wesley's hymnbook shows the horrible condition of the modern Jew.

> Outcasts from thee, and scatter'd wide
>   Through every nation under heaven,
> Blaspheming whom they crucified,
>   Unsaved, unpitied, unforgiving,
> Branded like Cain, they bear their load,
>   Abhor'd of men, and cursed of God.[31]

23. Ibid., 528.

24. Ibid., 46.

25. Ibid., 263.

26. Ibid., 524.

27. Ibid., 255.

28. Ibid., 306.

29. Ibid., 54.

30. Ibid., 303.

31. Wesley, *Wesley's Hymns*, no. 451, v. 2.

JUDAISM AND SALVATION

The question then arises as to whether or not the Jews will be saved. They have been the recipients of the first oracles of God, they have been under the first covenant of God, and they have been the people of God. Are they, then, to be dismissed or to be saved now that the second dispensation has been given to mankind?

The Jew, like the Christian, is to be saved by his faith. Wesley clearly finds evidence in Paul to back this idea. In commenting upon the doctrine of Sin, he writes:

> Is not his (Paul's) main point throughout that chapter (Rom 4) to prove, that both Jews and Gentiles were "justified by faith?" or, is he "speaking this, not of mankind in general, but of the Gentiles only [parentheses mine]!" "He proceeds: (Rom 5:1): 'Therefore, being justified by faith, we,' Gentiles, 'have peace with God.'" In the same manner you thrust in the word Gentiles into each of the following verses. Had then the Gentiles only "peace with God?" You might with more colour have inserted Jews in every verse; for of them chiefly the Apostle had been speaking.?[32]

This same idea is clearly found in many other places in Wesley's writings.

Wesley has no doubt but that when the full number of Gentiles has come into the saving relationship with God, the Jews will then return.[33] The Jew, like the Gentile, must receive God's mercies by faith.[34] The Jews received the first offer of salvation from God. "*He also is a son of Abraham*—A Jew born, and as such has a right to the first offer of salvation."[35] God's mercy is shown towards the Jew,[36] for he is to receive the gospel.[37]

> Come, then, thou great Deliverer, come!
>   The veil from Jacob's heart remove'
> Receive thy ancient people home!
>   That, quicken'd by thy dying love,
> The world may their reception find
> Life from the dead for all mankind.[38]

32. Wesley, *Works*, 9:269–70.

33. Ibid.

34. Wesley, *Notes*, 690.

35. Ibid., 274.

36. Ibid., 531.

37. Ibid., 519.

38. Wesley, *Wesley's Hymns*, no. 451, v. 4.

Again, the early Methodist sang of the Jew:

> To save the race forlorn,
>   Thy glorious arm display!
> And show the world's nation born,
>   A nation in a day![39]

By their response of faith both Jew and Gentile seek salvation through the various dispensations of God. Both must trust God for their salvation, and they must come to Him expecting and hoping to receive His mercy.

> . . . neither the Gentiles by the law of nature, nor the Jews by the law of Moses, could obtain justification before God' and . . . therefore it was necessary for both to seek it from the free mercy of God by faith: (2) that God has an absolute right to show mercy on what terms He pleases, and to withhold it from those who will not accept it on His own terms.[40]

The Jew is to be saved, but it is a salvation by faith.[41] Not only is faith a requirement, but also the Jew is to show more evidences in his life. We found the Jew falling down at this point, as far as Wesley was concerned. They were not being taught by the inspiration of God, not loving God as they ought, not loving their neighbor as they ought, and not turning to God. Therefore, according to Wesley, these are the points at which a Jew ought to be extremely careful and fulfill them in his life, in order to be saved.[42]

There are no doubts in Wesley's mind but that God will accept some of the Jews. A letter to Ann Golton in 1786 concerns one under the Jewish dispensation.

> There can be no possible reason to doubt concerning the happiness of that child. He did fear God, and according to his circumstances work righteousness. This is the essence of religion, according to St. Peter. His soul, therefore, was "darkly safe with God," although he was only under the Jewish Dispensation.[43]

Again we find that the Jew is saved by faith, the faith of the Jewish dispensation. Notice, that this is a modern Jew that Wesley is discussing.

39. Ibid., no. 450, v. 4.
40. Wesley, *Notes*, 514.
41. Ibid., 280.
42. Wesley, *Works*, 8:191–92.
43. Wesley, *Letters*, 7:358.

The modern Jew, as well as the ancient, is to work righteousness in his life if he is to be saved. This concept is found with Wesley in his dealings with all men.

The sacraments of the ancient Jew were effective and those participating received the grace of salvation.[44] Both the Jew and the Gentile may receive an infinitely greater reward than they deserve.[45] God's grace is freely given to both Jew and Gentile.

God is no respecter of persons, but will accept all believers. Those who accept His work of salvation are the "children of the promise," and those who do not accept His grace are those who are "children after the flesh."

> The sum is, God accepts all believers, and them only; and this is no way contrary to His word. Nay, He hath declared in His word, both by types and by express testimonies, that believers are accepted as the "children of the promise," while unbelievers are rejected, though they are "children after the flesh."[46]

Wesley finds evidence to believe with Paul, that when all is said and done, the Jews will come back into the saving relationship with God.[47] They will return when the quota of believing Gentiles has come in and the Jews provoked to jealousy. On the other hand, God is not the savior of the Jews alone, thereby showing that the Gentiles will return to God, and be saved as well as the Jews.[48]

Through the marvelous workings of God's grace, an unplumbed mystery to man, He has allowed both the Jews and the Gentiles to take their time in revolting against Himself. However, He has been, and is calling them back to Himself. This glorious work will only be "complete when they both return to Him, through the vehicle of faith."

> For God hath shut up all together in disobedience—Suffering each in their turn to revolt from Him. First, God suffered the Gentiles in the early age to revolt, and took the family of Abraham as a peculiar seed to Himself. Afterwards He permitted them to fall through unbelief, and took in the believing Gentiles. And He did even this to provoke the Jews to jealousy, and so bring them also in the end

44. Wesley, *Works*, 7:183.
45. Wesley, *Notes*, 97.
46. Ibid., 555–56.
47. Ibid., 565.
48. Ibid., 319.

to faith. This was truly a mystery in the divine conduct, which the apostle adores with such holy astonishment.[49]

This is enough to impress upon us the interest Wesley had in the salvation of the Jew. The Jew receives salvation through the forgiving grace of God, faith being the condition of his acceptance. As far as our judging at this point in time, we can only say with Wesley, "Yet it is not our part to pass sentence upon them, but to leave them to their own Master."[50]

JUDAISM AND CHRISTIANITY

The difference between a Jew and a Christian is quite large. Both receive freely the grace of God, both are related to God through a dispensation from Him, and both are saved by the condition of faith. At this point the difference ends. The Christian is in quite a different relationship with God than is the Jew. The possibilities of salvation for the two are not the same.

> Wesley pointed out that a greater measure of the Holy Spirit is accorded under the Christian than under the Jewish dispensation. The Christian's possibilities of salvation are quite other than those under the Jewish dispensation.[51]

The Christian and the Jew have the same God, but different relationships with Him. The Jew is accepted through his faith-response to God through the law and prophets, whereas the Christian is accepted through his faith-response to God through the revelation of Jesus Christ.

Wesley clarifies his thoughts a bit in his Articles of Religion, which were originally written by the Anglican Church and later accepted by the Methodist Church in America.

> The Old Testament is not contrary to the New; for both in the Old and New Testament everlasting life is offered to mankind by Christ, who is the only Mediator between God and man, being both God and Man. Wherefore they are not to be heard who feign that the old fathers did look only for transitory promises. Although the law given from God by Moses as touching ceremonies and rites doth not bind Christians, nor ought the civil precepts thereof of necessity be received in any commonality; yet notwithstanding,

---

49. Ibid., 567–68.

50. Wesley, *Works*, 7:198.

51. Lindstrom, *Wesley and Sanctification*, 135.

no Christian whatsoever is free from this obedience of the commandments which are called moral.[52]

The Christian is to convert the Jew. Since there is more of the Holy
Spirit available through the Christian dispensation, the Christian has more
light available to him. This light is to be shared with the Jew. The command-
ing center, the essence of Christian's light and the uniqueness of the dispensation given to him, is to be found in Jesus Christ, our Lord and Savior.

The wrong way for the Christian to work for this conversion of the
Jew is to allow the Jew to think that we believe the Messiah not to have
come, or that the Messiah is, after all, unnecessary. In other words, we are
not to collapse our Christianity. "It is converting them by allowing all that
they contend for, and by granting them the main point in question."[53]

The Christian dispensation supplanted the Jewish, and the Christian
religion is the fulfillment of Judaism. The "people of God" of the Jewish
dispensation, became the "people of God" under the new Christian dispensation. The Christian became the true seed of Abraham, the new Israel.
Christianity supplanted Judaism.

Wesley discusses these things in a long passage in the *Notes*,[54] in
which he talks about the term, "God's elect." God called the Jews. Various
names were ascribed to them, arising from this unique relationship, such
as: "the children of God," "the sons of God," "holy people," "a chosen seed,"
"the elect," "the called of God," and others. Due to the unique relationship of the Jew to God, these and other terms were used to describe this
dispensation of God.

Christ and His followers arose out of Judaism. They were the fulfillment of Judaism—its completeness as well as its fulfillment. Those who
accepted Christ, both Jews and Gentiles, have become "God's elect." Those
in the old Jewish dispensation, who did not accept Him, became numbered
among the reprobate. All the terms that applied to the old dispensation
were now given to the new one, which God worked through Christ.[55]

The reason for such usage of language was the first calling of the
Israelites by God, from among the people of the earth. This unusual and
unique relationship was given many titles and meanings as the Jews be-

52. *Book of Discipline*, 103.

53. Wesley, *Letters*, 3:345.

54. Wesley, *Notes*, 552.

55. Ibid., 522.

came more familiar with their God and His mighty acts. The names were used in the new relationship, made available by God through His Son, Jesus Christ, when the old dispensation gave way to the new.

> God's electing or choosing the nation of Israel, and separating them from the other nations, who were sunk in idolatry and all wickedness, gave the first occasion to this sort of language. And as the separating the Christians from the Jews was a like event, no wonder it was expressed in like words and phrases: only with this difference, the term elect was of old applied to all the members of the visible Church; whereas in the New Testament it is applied only to the members of the invisible.[56]

Argument could be made for the special condition and advantage of the Jews from the Articles of Religion, which Wesley sent to the Methodist Church in America. The sixth article states "they are not to be heard who feign that the old fathers did look only for transitory promises."

Wesley seems to be of the opinion that the Jews occupy a high place in God's grace. The Jew sees that God is holy, and finds the spiritual meaning of the law. His sin is laid bare before him and he knows he deserves punishment at the hands of God. The anguish of a wounded spirit is his continual accompaniment. He struggles to rid himself of his sin, but the stronger he struggles the tighter the net of sin is drawn around him.

> Thus he toils without end, repenting and sinning, and repenting and sinning again, till at length the poor, sinful, helpless wretch is even at his wit's end, and can barely groan "O wretched man that I am! Who shall deliver me from the body of this death?"[57]

Wesley gives a quick summary of the various conditions of men before God. In it he portrays the condition of the Heathen to be that of a man who has neither fear nor love for God. The Jew, on the other hand, has progressed beyond that. The Jew is under the law—his is a spirit of bondage, he has the fear of God. The Christian is in the best condition, as the three stand before God, for the Christian has passed from the spirit of bondage to the spirit of adoption by God and lives in the love of God as a son.

56. Ibid., 553.
57. Wesley, *Works*, 5:104.

> The heathen, baptized or unapprised, hath a fancied liberty, which is indeed licentiousness; the Jew, or one under the Jewish dispensation, is in heavy, grievous bondage; the Christian enjoys the true glorious liberty of the sons of God.[58]

The Jew is not under the same condition as the Christian. His position is inferior, for he has not the depth of the relationship to God that has become the gift of God to the Christian. Arguing from the Epistle to the Hebrews, Wesley says:

> ... that Christians are under a better covenant, established upon better promises; that although "the law made nothing perfect," made none perfect either in holiness or happiness, yet "the bringing in of a better hope" did, "by which we" now "draw nigh unto God,"—this is the great truth continually inculcated herein, and running through this whole Epistle.[59]

The 1780 hymnbook contains an interesting song with lyrics that lead one to believe the Jews will one day return. God, having given His call first to them, will not let the promise remain unfulfilled:

> We know it must be done,
>   For God hath spoke the word:
> All Israel shall the Saviour own,
>   To their first state restored:
> Rebuilt by his command,
>   Jerusalem shall rise:
> Her temple on *Moriah* stand
>   Again, and touch the skies.[60]

58. Ibid., 5:108.
59. Wesley, *Journal*, 3:50.
60. Wesley, *Wesley's Hymns*, no. 452, v. 4.

4

Deism and "True Christianity"

W E NOW EMBARK UPON a quite different line of thought. We have been considering other religions, their relationship to Christianity, and the possibility of gaining salvation through them.

Now we deal with those who consider themselves to be Christians. The distinction here drawn is between Wesley's conception of real or True Christianity, and the Christianity portrayed by these others.

Wesley is sure that at many points in their thoughts, the Deists are no better than Heathens or others entirely outside the Christian dispensation. As far as Deism is concerned, he seems to think it utterly foreign to Christianity, as he knows and preaches it. Let us begin by defining Deism.

THE DEFINITION OF DEISM

In the *Encyclopedia of Religion*, Deism is defined this way:

> The term *deism* was originally equivalent to *theism*, differing only in etymology: theism based on the Greek word for god (*theos*), and deism on the Latin *(deus)*. In the seventeenth and eighteenth centuries, however, deism came to signify one or another form of rationalistic theological unorthodoxy.... In its principal meaning, deism signifies the belief in a single God and in a religious practice founded solely on natural reason rather than on supernatural revelation.... Deism was most prominent in England, the only place where it approached the status of a movement. Among its best-known representatives were Lord Hertbert of Cherbury (1583–1648) . . . Charles Blount (1654–1693) . . . John Toland (1670–1722) . . . Anthony Collins (1676–1729) . . . Matthew Tindal (1657–1733)[1]

---

1. Wood, *"Deism,"* 2251.

This gives us one point of view, but the historian and theologian Arthur W. Nagler clarified Deism for us.

> . . . contended for a natural religion which all rational men might accept, in consequence of which many traditions, doctrines, and practices of the historic church were summarily cast aside as so much worthless rubble. Naturally, although we now see the weaknesses and some of the . . . Deistic contentions, the Christian apologists of the day . . . felt that Christianity must be shown to be reasonable, a faith that could be logically demonstrated and is to be accepted on that score.[2]

We now turn to the common views of Deism during Wesley's time, and particularly to his analysis of its meaning.

Cannon has collected the five principles that Lord Herbert of Cherbury set forth as points common to all men. First, is their belief in one supreme God. Second, this supreme God is the one who ought to be worshipped by all men. Third, the two chief parts of worshipping this God are virtue and piety. Fourth, we ought to be sorry for the sins that we have committed, and repent of them. Fifth, the goodness of God relates to man by His giving rewards and punishments to men, both in this life and the life to come.[3]

I think that upon consideration, we will find that Deism is quite a full and involved system that is arrayed against the whole Christian system. It is one system, Christianity, in conflict with another, Deism, not just the disagreement of two competing ideas within a single system such as would be the case if the Methodists and Presbyterians were to discuss their differing issues. This is the contention of Wesley, and his position seems to be borne out if we take a closer look.

Take, for instance, the fact that both believe in one supreme God. However, we must remember that the interpretation of the two systems concerning this God and His activities may vary extremely. Again, the manner of knowing and relating oneself to this God will vary. Just because they are united in their contention that there is one God of the universe, does not mean that their beliefs about this God are the same—in fact they differ widely and radically.

---

2. Nagler, *Church in History*, 186.

3. Cannon, *Theology of John Wesley*, 17; Latourette, *History of Christianity*, 1004; Nagler, *Church in History*, 186.

Or again, consider the fact that both think this God ought to be worshipped. Both commonly accept the fact of worship, but the manner in which man is to worship is quite different. The True Christian worships God through all of the means of grace that God has given. The Deist may not think that the means of grace are necessary elements for man's worship of God. The Deist thinks piety and virtue are the two requirements for man to worship God, whereas the True Christian thinks differently. These doctrinal differences will be examined in some detail later.

Both believe that man ought to be sorry for the sins that he has committed. We see the commonness here, but what is considered to be the essence of sin? The two widely differ in their interpretation of sin and its meanings with respect to man's life and his relationship with God. The True Christian believes man to be more deeply involved in sin and estranged from God, than does the Deist.

The truth of the situation is as Cannon says, the Deists " . . . in reality . . . maintain that the Christian revelation is not necessary."[4] This says about as much about Wesley as it does about the Deist. This may not be the best definition, but it does serve to point out some distinctions between the two, particularly as Wesley understood them. Even further, he finds two radically different types of Deists, though they are united in their adherence to Deism.

> One sort are more beasts in human shape, wholly under the power of the basest passions, and having "a downright appetite to mix with mud." Other Deists are, in most respects, rational creatures, though unhappily prejudiced against Christianity. Most of these believe the being and attributes of God; they believe that God made and governs the world; and that the soul does not die with the body, but will remain for ever in a state of happiness or misery.[5]

An interesting observation at this point is to note how little Wesley really deals with Deism, which many would consider to be the largest plague erected against True Christianity during that century. Cannon helps us understand the significance of this fact.[6] W. T. Watkins also helps, "John Wesley did not refute Deism. He was far too busy helping men find

---

4. Cannon, *Theology of John Wesley*, 97.

5. Wesley, *Works*, 7:196.

6. Cannon, *Theology of John Wesley*, 20.

God to bother with the theory that he (God) could not be found [parentheses mine]."[7]

Wesley did not make a direct, frontal, or intellectual attack upon the tenets of Deism, one book following another in quick succession. He did not fight the philosophical Deism with a better philosophy, constructed upon his Christian convictions. Instead, he was almost strangely silent upon the whole matter. However we dare not think that he was letting sleeping dogs lie.

For us to understand the manner by which Wesley was continually attacking Deism, we must remember that Deism had nothing to do with revelation, reason being a chief foundation and cornerstone. Wesley entirely differed from this tenet, being biblically based in his thought. His line of attack is to make his own biblically based convictions as strong as possible, and by presenting them in this manner, attack the Deist menace. Instead of entering into a slugfest with those leaders, he presented his own position to the best possible advantage and let this method carry the bulk of the fight.

> The surest way to bring deists to Christianity, thought Wesley, was not by argument but by living example, by the positive affirmation of the principles of the Bible in character and in life. The aim of the Wesleyan Revival, therefore, was to establish biblical Christianity over the land. Reason was not the mistress of revelation; revelation itself was the starting point, for God had made his will known to man and had called on man for loyalty and allegiance.[8]

Wesley and the Wesleyan revival met the danger of this philosophical aberration of Christianity by delivering a straightforward presentation of their view. Against the new barriers of reason set free, a "universal" religion of man, etc. . . . Wesley set the timeless faith of the Christian Church, the revelation of God as found in Jesus Christ.

> To this groping age Wesley declared that those whose sins God forgives, he assures by an inner voice that they are his children. This fellowship with God was not simply a testimony about a transaction over with and finished in the forgiveness of sins but was a daily communion in which men found an uplift that changed life from a monotonous, commonplace plodding into a glorious, eter-

7. Watkins, *Out of Aldersgate*, 93.
8. Cannon, *Theology of John Wesley*, 20.

nally alluring pilgrimage. It was God's grace constantly available to men, daily endowing them with strength for the work of life.[9]

In the preface to his *Standard Sermons*, Wesley points out his foundation upon the Scripture for his study and work. The Scriptures are the foundation upon which he builds the rule he uses to measure his thought and conduct.

> I have accordingly set down in the following sermons what I find in the Bible concerning the way to heaven; with a view to distinguish this was of God from all those which are the inventions of men. I have endeavored to describe the true, the scriptural, experimental religion, so as to omit nothing which is a real part thereof, and to add nothing thereto which is not.[10]

Founded squarely upon Scripture, Wesley sought with all use of reason possible to explain and defend his interpretations of the meanings of God, man, and the relationship existing between them, which by God's grace, has been made possible.

Wesley attacked Dr. Conyers Middleton, for exchanging the birthright of Christianity for the pottage of Deism. The manner in which Dr. Middleton interpreted original sin and other doctrines was enough to convince Wesley that Christianity was being undermined and would not recover from such interpretations, if they went unchecked.

One of the points of controversy between them concerned the external evidence of Christianity. Wesley was almost willing to give up the evidences of Christianity, in their external form (i.e., miracles and such), suggesting that they were always the weaker arguments. He thought that the most basic and convincing evidences were the internal. The internal evidence ". . . and every true believer hath the witness or evidence in himself . . ."[11] the "light shining in their hearts,"[12] is by far superior to any argument or external form that can be presented.

> What Christianity (considered as a doctrine) promised is accomplished in my soul. And Christianity, considered as an inward principle, is the completion of all those promises. It is holiness and

9. Watkins, *Out of Aldersgate*, 93–94.

10. Wesley, *Works*, 5:4.

11. Wesley, *Letters*, 2:384.

12. Ibid., 2:385.

happiness the image of God impressed on a created spirit, a foun-
tain of peace and love springing up into everlasting life.[13]

By his Deistic interpretation, Wesley wonders why Dr. Middleton
even wants to continue to be called a Christian. The word means nothing because the reality of his thought is so different from that of a True
Christian. He does not have the inner evidence of Christianity within his
life, so there is little reason to contend for his being a Christian. What may
be called "Christian," is found in his opinions, but not in his life.

> May I without offence ask of you that are called Christians, What real
> loss would you sustain in giving up your present opinion that the
> Christian system is of God? Though you bear the name, you are not
> Christians: you have neither Christian faith nor love. You have no
> divine evidence of things unseen; you have not entered into the holi-
> est by the blood of Jesus. . . . Does not the main of your Christianity
> lie in your opinion, decked with a few outward observances?[14]

This passage follows nine and one-half pages in which Wesley presents
his own views as to who is a Christian, the fundamentals of Christianity,
and what the Christian faith entails. It likewise follows sixty-two pages in
which he takes, point-by-point, the thesis of Dr. Middleton and argues
against them. Therefore, this is not just a passage of idle moments—he
had few enough of them to spare—but a thought-out presentation of his
position.

Sugden points out the effect of this Deistical movement when he
first quotes William Edward Hartpole Lecky and then Dr. William John
Townsend:

> ". . . to lower enthusiasm and to diminish superstition. Men become
> half believers. Strong religious passions of all kinds died away" . . .
> "The sentiments and principles of the Deists gained multitudes of
> adherents. The wits, beaus, and rakes of the fashionable world gladly
> availed themselves of teachings which relaxed the bonds of morality
> and permitted greater license of conduct."[15]

---

13. Ibid., 2:383.

14. Ibid., 2:385.

15. Wesley, *Standard Sermons*, 2:435–36.

THE DEISTIC FAILURE

Deism was presented by some of its enthusiastic followers as the only alternative for the futility of Papism, which we would call Roman Catholicism today. This hidden persuader Wesley was not willing to accept. The situation was more complex than this, he believed, for some were neither Roman Catholics nor Deists.

> It may be doubted whether Deism is the sole expedient to secure us against popery; for some are of opinion there are persons in the world who are neither Deists nor Papists.[16]

This subtle approach being repelled, we now dig further into Wesley's controversy with the Deists, and find the failures of Deism, as he presents them.

In his sermon, "On Faith," Wesley charges the Deists with having no God. Their position is a distinct denial of God, because it is an undermining of the whole Christian foundation. Virtue is to be sought after by the Deist, but it is of a strange kind. The more a man's benevolent actions are done from the desire to please God, the less virtue is to be found within them, from the Deist point of view. Wesley quotes William Wollaston in answer to the question: "Does the having an eye to God in an action enhance the virtue of it?"

> No; it is so far from this, that if in doing a virtuous, that is, a benevolent, action, a man mingles a desire to please God, the more there is of this desire, the less virtue there is in that action.[17]

It is no wonder that Wesley comments: "Never before did I meet with either, Jew, Turk or Heathen who so flatly renounced God as this Christian professor!"

The next failure of Deists is their tendency to reason beyond what man may rightfully know. God has revealed all that is necessary for the salvation of man. Man's reasoning beyond that which is given by God, in the order of salvation, is utter folly. Yet, man has so done, and in doing this, he has fallen heir to the Deistic failure.

> I believe that most of the controversies which have disturbed the Church have arisen from people's wanting to be wise above what is written, not contented with what God has plainly revealed there

16. Wesley, *Letters*, 2:313.
17. Wesley, *Works*, 7:201.

> ... I dare not, will not, reason about it for a moment. I believe just
> what is revealed and no more. But I do not pretend to account for
> it, or to solve the difficulties that may attend it. Let angels do this,
> if they can. But I think they cannot.[18]

With this danger goes the similar one of connecting events together
wrongfully, which may likewise lead to Deism.[19] Wesley speaks of some
who say they are as sure that a particular action is God's will, as that they
are just. Also, some say, "God as surely spoke this to my heart as ever He
spoke to me at all." This type of connecting events together frightened the
mind of Wesley, even though he was prone to do it himself.[20]

In a 1756 letter to William Law, Wesley wrote in regard to some philosophical leanings and mistakes that he felt needed correction. Though
Law, later in his life, is chiefly known to have become over influenced by
the Mystic writers, at this point Wesley attacks him on the same grounds
as he does the Deists. From this attack, we might learn much about how
Wesley opposed the Deistic arguments.

The first failure, with which Wesley charges Law, is that he denies
the omnipotence of God. His philosophical floundering and speculations
lead Law into some pretty peculiar statements. For example, Wesley comments upon Law's idea concerning the body:

> Astonishing! What a discovery is this, that a body is only a curdled
> spirit! That our bodies are only the sum total of our spiritual prop-
> erties! And that the form of every man's body is only the form of
> his spirit made visible![21]

Law will not allow that God can change the creation; it must have been
created in the form we now find it. He has no room for continued changes
within the order of creation; that which was at first created an ox remains
forever an ox. If a man is to be an angel in his final life, he must have been
created an angel in the first place. Wesley then comments:

> But what divinity! and what reasoning to support it! Can God
> raise nothing higher than its first created state? ... Poor omnipo-
> tence which cannot do this! Whether He will or no is another

18. Wesley, *Letters*, 8:89.

19. Ibid., 7:263.

20. Ibid.

21. Ibid., 3:344.

question. . . . Thus does your attachment to a miserable philosophy lead you to deny the almighty power of God.[22]

To a man who put his signature to such verses as 1 and 2 of hymn 234 in the 1779 hymnbook, it is impossible to be reconciled to the view here suggested:

> He spake the word, and it was done!
>> The universe his Word obey'd;
> His Word is his eternal Son,
>> And Christ the whole creation made.

The two interpretations are irreconcilable. Or again, one might find other evidence in the hymnbook.[23] Finally, such verses as this entirely forbid it:

> In earth, in heaven, in all thou art;
>> The conscious creature feels thy nod,
> Whose forming hand on every part
>> Impress'd the image of its God.[24]

At this point, we find the Deistic frown upon the miracles and other supernatural qualities of Christianity. The miraculous elements are extremely soft-pedaled and man's natural qualities are sounded forth with trumpet blast with the entire proper accompaniment.

The second failure that Wesley charges Law of committing is that his doctrine denies the justice of God, which in effect, denies His power as well. Wesley considers this to be one of the great turning points between Deism and Christianity. This is the point at which Christianity must not back down, or the contention of Deism is made solid and that of Christianity, like the house built upon the sand, would fall. The doctrine of God's justice is the proper foundation of that of the Atonement, etc. If this, the foundation be given away, the whole structure built upon it must likewise fall.

> . . . it is now one main hinge on which the controversy between Christianity and Deism turns. To convert a thousand Deists, therefore, by giving up this point, with the doctrine of Justification which is built upon it, is little more than it would be to convert as many Jews by allowing the Messiah is not yet come. It is converting

---

22. Ibid., 3:344–45.

23. Wesley, *Wesley's Hymns*, no. 242–44.

24. Ibid., no. 241, v. 1.

them by allowing all they contend for, by granting them the main point in question. Consequently it is no other than establishing Deism while it pretends to overturn it.[25]

Wesley quotes Scripture in support of this contention that God is just. He shows how Law, in this work "Spirit of Love," denies Wesley's contention.[26] Law does not take the wrath of God literally or seriously and assumes that others would not take it literally, either. Properly speaking, he can find no such thing, which leaves Wesley quite at odds with him.

As in his other arguments with the Deists, Wesley attempts to remain firm in his foundation upon the Scripture and not budge an inch from this basis. From this foundation, he builds his theology and attacks those who differ. He summarizes the work of Law in this manner:

> You say: (1) There is no vindictive, avenging, or punitive justice in God. (2) There is no wrath or anger in God. (3) God inflicts no punishment on any creature, neither in this world nor that to come.[27]

Now Wesley quotes Scripture, God's word, in support of his position. He gives seven passages to refute the first contention of Law, twenty-seven to refute the second, and seven on the third. This seems to be enough backing for his point and he then goes on to other differences.

The real point of the difficulty is found and stated so well by Cannon when he writes:

> In the last analysis . . . the Bible is for Wesley the way to religious knowledge and to a comprehension of truth concerning God and God's relation to man. To be sure, reason is an essential tool for the interpretation of the Bible, and Wesley writes that he builds all his religious opinions on Scripture as he interprets it through the means of common sense.[28]

The Deists based their thoughts upon other presuppositions, other limits of significance, and thought that by so doing they were able to reason without faith. Wesley found his faith in scriptural Christianity, granted

25. Wesley, *Letters*, 3:345.
26. Ibid.
27. Ibid., 3:350.
28. Cannon, *Theology of John Wesley*, 160.

the Deists this point, and from his position he reasoned as sharply and well as any man.

DEISM AND SALVATION

As far as salvation is concerned, we find scant evidence in the writings of Wesley as to whether the Deists are to be saved or not. We can break some ground and consider a few of Wesley's comments, which though they may not be exactly to the point, offer acceptable evidence.

"The Savannah Journal," written early in his career, gives us some interesting information. He was considering the case of the Roman Catholics and the Deists, with reference to the hardness of converting each of them to Christianity, as he believed it. The condition of each is hazardous and dangerous at best, but he recognized a hierarchy of danger. The Roman Catholic is closest, the Deist next, and the infidel the furthest away from True Christianity. At this time he had never seen a Deist reconverted to the true tenets of Christianity, though he was later to know John Frederick Lampe, John Walsh, and other Deists who were reconverted.[29]

We would do well to consider the degrees of danger so illustrated by the Roman Catholic and Deist with the True Christian. As bad as he thought a Roman Catholic was, as we will find in the next chapter, the infidel or Deist was much more a child of hell than any Catholic he had met.[30]

> ... (2) because as dangerous a state as a Papist is in, with regard to eternity, a Deist is in a far more dangerous state, if he be not (without repentance) an assured heir of damnation; and (3) because as difficult as it is to recover a Papist, 'tis far more difficult to recover an Infidel.[31]

We see well here the dangerous circumstance of the Deists, as described by Wesley. It seems that the Deist occupies the same place as an infidel in Wesley's mind, at least at this point in his career.

I think Lindstrom's emphasis upon the pull of Wesley's theology towards the doctrine of sanctification is worthy of consideration at this point of our discussion. Wesley thought that we ought to grow in our apprehension of the truth and especially grow on from faith to faith. Man is created so he should and could grow from stage to stage in faith. This is

29. Wesley, *Journal*, 1:358.
30. Ibid.
31. Ibid.

what sanctification following justification is all about. Sanctification is the continued growth of the Christian in the faith.

If we remember this goal in Wesley's theology, we may well contend that the faith of the Deists makes sense within the framework of the order of salvation, if it is outgrown as one presses for more light. In the area of doctrine, he pronounces the Deists entirely wrong, from the basis of their faith throughout the whole foundation raised upon it. In the order of salvation, I think that we can hold out some hope for them.

> There is no reason why you should be satisfied with the faith of a Materialist, Heathen, or a Deist; nor, indeed, with that of a servant. I do not know that God requires it at your hands. Indeed, if you have received this, you ought not to cast it away; you ought not in anywise to undervalue it; but to be truly thankful for it. Yet, in the mean time, beware how you rest here: Press on till you receive the Spirit of adoption: Rest not, till that Spirit clearly witnesses with your spirit, that you are a child of God.[32]

In his sermon "On Faith" Wesley places the faith of a Deist above that of a materialist, but below that of a Heathen or Mohammedan. Wesley thinks the Deist is a servant of God, though not yet receiving the spirit of sonship, which cannot be received until one has grown into the fullness of the faith.

Though Wesley points to the dangers inherent in Deism, uncovers Deist weaknesses, and their path trod by the precipice of condemnation, still he does not call for the final blow of condemnation for them. He does not strictly condemn them. He is strangely silent upon this point. In all of the other positions taken he gives a treatment full enough that we can find where the faith of a Deist stands, yet on this one we do not find enough material.

It might be possible for us to assume that the Deist will be tried like the Heathen and the other, by the light which they have received, and their faithfulness to this light. Yet, we must remember that Wesley does not make a statement concerning them in the order of salvation. That is, other than the statement that they need not stop, but ought to grow on in the faith, to the goal of every man, complete sanctification, he offers nothing. They are under the spirit of bondage, the servants of God, this he

---

32. Wesley, *Works*, 7:200.

freely states. Yet, he does not finally seal their doom, by explicitly stating their condition to be utterly unsalvageable.

DEISM AND "TRUE CHRISTIANITY"

J. L. Neve gives his estimate of the Deist position in his book, *A History of Christian Thought*, by combining the work of Matthew Tindal with that of Thomas Chubb. Wesley knew Tindal and violently disagreed with him, so it would seem possible for us to be on common ground with Wesley after reading the Deist approach to Christianity through these two men.

Tindal thought that Christianity was another name for natural religion, meaning that faith is based upon natural reason rather than natural revelation. If Christianity was not synonymous with natural religion, it was going too far, bursting the prescribed boundaries. From this agreement with natural religion, it stepped out into the arena of superstition and the corruption of real religion.[33]

These men sought the fundamentals, which they believed to be common in all religions and mankind—past, present, or future. We have already seen a similar combination in Lord Herbert of Cherbury's five points, presented at the beginning of this chapter.

The addition of Chubb to Tindal comes in the form of the teachings of Jesus. Jesus came not to give His life for men, not to teach the doctrines of the Father, or even to lead men into a saving relationship with God. Jesus came to teach the simple lesson of the moral law. If the moral law, or conscience of men, has been violated, the natural response of man was to feel sorry and change his behavior. This is the meaning of salvation, but certainly not some mysterious divinity about *The Person And Place of Jesus Christ*, as so aptly written by P. T. Forsyth.[34]

> ...he aimed to show that Christ had wanted to teach simply the moral law, the "law of reason," the "law of nature." Christianity is simply the religion of obeying the moral law or the dictates of the conscience. If this law has been violated, then there must be repentance and reform, which will be followed by divine forgiveness. This is the whole doctrine of salvation.[35]

33. Neve, *History of Christian Thought*, 2:61.

34. Forsyth, *Person and Place of Jesus*.

35. Neve, *History of Christian Thought*, 2:61.

It appears to me that we have abundant evidence to show why Wesley and the Deists could not find common ground. The strong point in Wesley's theology, the area of his major concentration and concern, is the order of salvation. In the development of this doctrine, he spent almost his entire adult life.

This weak point in the Deist framework is precisely the strong point in Wesley—the doctrine of salvation. Wesley could not long stand by and let the strong, the central, and the key elements of Christianity, as he knew it, be trampled upon by the Deists. Though he did not give much of a frontal attack, in the form of books, lectures, and pamphlets, for him to preach on any subject within the order of salvation, was in reality, an attack upon the Deists.

Wesley's concern from the early years of his life was salvation. This was the thirst that led him through the tumultuous early years, and the finding of the saving relationship that was the burden of his message throughout the remaining ones. He must have studied and worked this doctrine through multitudes of times. He was forever preaching upon the theme and has left, as a heritage to those within the Church he founded, a remarkable life-long contribution of thought and works upon this doctrine. Wesley didn't enter into a clash of name calling, he didn't rant and rave, but every time he mounted the pulpit, it was a clarion call to the True Christianity rather than the watered down version given by the Deists. The *Standard Sermons* are evidence enough of this. We have only to look at the sermon titles to find our answer: "Salvation By Faith," "Scriptural Christianity," "Justification By Faith," "The Righteousness Of Faith," "The Way To The Kingdom," "The First-Fruits Of The Spirit," "The Spirit Of Bondage And Of Adoption," "The Means Of Grace," "The Circumcision Of The Heart," "The Marks Of The New Birth," "Christian Perfection," "Original Sin," "The New Birth," "The Wilderness State," and given by Sugden in addition, "The Witness Of The Spirit," "On Sin In Believers," "The Repentance Of Believers," "The Lord Our Righteousness," and "The Scripture Way Of Salvation." Almost any sermon in the "Standards" would be usable against the contentions of the Deists.

Wesley could not believe that the Deists were Christian. Their beliefs rotted the foundations of Christianity, and were what the natural man would most like to hear and believe. The Deists were something separate and apart from True Christianity, they had a different spirit.

The main point of contention comes with the Christian doctrine of the Atonement. For the Deist, this is like trying to squeeze a camel through the eye of a needle, and for Wesley, this is the most viral and important point of scriptural Christianity. Were this point not granted, there would be no use for the remainder of Christianity.

In a letter to Mary Bishop, February 7, 1778, Wesley states his position concisely. He begins by telling her that it is not important whether she became confused in reading William Law, or talking with another of the Deists. It is the truth of the doctrine of the Atonement that is the important consideration.

> Indeed, nothing in the Christian system is of greater consequence then the doctrine of Atonement. It is properly the distinguishing point between Deism and Christianity. "The scriptural scheme of morality," said Lord Huntingdon, "is what every one must admire; but the doctrine of Atonement I cannot comprehend." Here, then, we divide. Give up the Atonement, and the Deists are agreed with us.[36]

Wesley then refers Miss Bishop to his letter written to Mr. Law, encourages her to read this letter, and in this manner to find more light upon this grand doctrine. Then he continues:

> But it is true I can no more *comprehend* it than his lordship; perhaps I might say than the angels of God, than the highest created understanding. Our *reason* is here quickly bewildered. If we attempt to expatiate in this *field*, we "find no end, in wandering mazes lost."[37]

At this point, Wesley draws more inferences from the doctrine of the atonement. If God was never angry with them, there would have been no need for reconciliation, and by Mr. Law's affirming this very thing, Wesley finds him striking at the whole foundation of the doctrine. His letter to Law reflects these feelings on the matter.

By his own experience, Wesley believes that he knew God as an angry judge. God's anger continued in Wesley's life until he came to a saving-faith in Christ. It was only then that reconciliation took place, by the merits of Christ being applied personally to him.

---

36. Wesley, *Letters*, 6:297–98.

37. Ibid., 6:298.

This does not mean that the doctrine of the atonement will have no further problems. As long as there are men there will be misunderstandings and objections to it.

> For still the preaching of Christ crucified will be foolishness to the wise men of the world. However, let us hold the precious truth fast in our heart as well as in our understanding; and we shall find by happy experience that this is to us the wisdom of God and the power of God.[38]

This conclusion could well be read and taken to heart by the ministers of our day. It carries a needed message that one does not often hear from the pulpit.

From this, and the proceeding sections, I think enough material is presented to understand the immense differences between Deism and True Christianity. This philosophical aberration differs from Christianity from the very foundation. Christianity is founded upon the work of Christ and the atonement that is thereby won. Deism is founded upon the commonness of all religion and the use of reason rather than revelation.

Alexander Pope offered his take on Deism in verse:

> All nature is but Art unknown to thee;
> All chance direction, which thou canst not see;
> All discord, harmony not understood;
> All partial evil, universal good;
> And spite of Pride, in erring Reason's spite,
> One truth is clear, *Whatever is, is right.*[39]

And turning to song, Wesley urged against the Pope's summary:

> O for a thousand tongues to sing
>   My great Redeemer's praise,
> The glories of my God and King,
>   The triumphs of His grace!
>
> He breaks the power of canceled sin,
>   He sets the prisoner free;
> His blood can make the foulest clean;
>   His blood availed for me.
>
> He speaks, and, listening to His voice,

---

38. Ibid., 6:298–99.

39. Norwood, *Development of Modern Christianity*, 118–19.

New life the dead receive;
The mournful, broken hearts rejoice;
The humble poor believe.[40]

There is a vast difference between the Deism that Wesley attacks and the Christianity he seeks to teach. The man who could agree with the following lyrics could not become a Deist, at least on the point of atonement, which was, after all, a watershed between the thought of the two:

O Love Divine! What hast thou done!
The immortal God hath died for me!
The Father's co-eternal Son
Bore all my sins upon the tree:
The immortal God for me hath died;
My Lord, my Love is crucified.[41]

40. *The United Methodist Hymnal*, no. 162.
41. Wesley, *Wesley's Hymns,* no. 28, v. 1.

Roman Catholicism and "True Christianity"

T HE POSSIBILITIES OF THIS topic are nearly endless and would require many hundreds of pages to properly write and document. Therefore, in such space limitations as this, the topic cannot be fully covered. We must limit our comments instead to the areas deemed most important in the theological outlook of Wesley.

THE ROMAN CATHOLIC FAILURE

Let us examine the meaning of the Roman Catholic Church, as we find it given and understood by Wesley in his "A Roman Catechism."

Q. What is the Church of Rome?

A. The Church of Rome is that Society of Christians which professes it necessary to salvation to be subject to the Pope of Rome, as the alone visible head of the Church.[1]

This is the Church with which Wesley has such differences, and yet he considers the Catholic Church to be one of a worldwide fellowship of Christians.

In order to understand Wesley's position we must first state that he declares that he has no desire for persecuting a man merely because he is a Roman Catholic. It is quite well known that Wesley is much more liberal than many of his day, concerning nonviolence and denial of persecution of Catholicism.[2] We have also studied his thinking about and treatment toward people who believe other religions.

He was sure that the number of converts to infidelity was much higher than those to the Roman Church. Also, he was convinced that "as bad as re-

1. Wesley, *Works*, 10:87.
2. Wesley, *Letters*, 6:371; Todd, *Wesley and the Catholic Church*, 9–27.

ligion as Popery is, no religion is still worse; a baptized infidel being always found, upon the trial, two-fold worse than even a bigoted Papist."[3]

The basis of his denial of persecution is that the Romans have the same Master as he, as well as the second argument and basic humane one, that Catholics are human beings.[4] Because of this double argument, he often speaks against any type of mistreatment of Roman Catholics.

Those who are less charitable in their dealings and writings against those of the Roman Church, he charges with a fundamental Christian lack of love or charity. Though he does not agree with the church in their doctrinal formulations,[5] he insists upon their fundamental right to believe differently in their opinions, without facing persecution for their efforts. Though they differ tremendously upon doctrine and opinion, they are Christian and ought to be treated with Christian charity.

> But I do not agree with the author of that tract ("A Seasonable Antidote against Popery") in the spirit of the whole performance [parentheses mine]. It does not seem to breathe either that modesty of seriousness or charity which one would desire. One would not desire to hear any private person, of no great note in the Church or the world, speak as it were ex cathedra, with an air of infallibility, or at least of vast self-sufficiency, on a point wherein men of eminence, both for piety, learning, and office, have been so greatly divided.[6]

The bone of contention between Wesley and the Roman Catholics is the definition of Christianity, not persecution. Indeed he will have nothing to do with persecution. In the 1780s Wesley continually pressed this point. During this period, the same point is urged in the "First Letter to the Freeman's Journal," "The Second Letter to the Freeman's Journal," "A Letter to the Printer of the 'Public Advertiser,'" and "A Disavowal of Persecuting Papists."[7] In "A Disavowal," Wesley says he "set out early in life with an utter abhorrence of persecution in every form, and a full conviction that every man has a right to worship God according to his own conscience."[8]

---

3. Wesley, *Works*, 1:50.
4. Wesley, *Letters*, 1:277–78; *Journal*, 1:263.
5. Wesley, *Works*, 6:84.
6. Wesley, *Letters*, 3:245.
7. Wesley, *Works*, 10:159–77.
8. Ibid., 10:173.

Certainly we here find a man of more vision and understanding than most of his contemporaries. The conclusion of the "Second Letter," is that he wishes freedom for the Romanists, but at the same time he wants them to be kept from undermining the freedom and liberties of the Protestants. They are not to be hurt, and in return are to be kept from hurting the Protestants.[9]

Wesley's view of *opinions* is here relevant. The concept of *opinions*, as used by Wesley, places them of lesser value than the more important concept, which is the concept of *doctrines*.[10] That is, Wesley never pours the complete content into the form of the doctrine. All must believe the brief outline of basic Christian beliefs, he teaches, but the means by which this framework is given life and completely sketched in might differ. Good Christians may differ upon opinions—this is their right. These opinions are not important for salvation. One must not necessarily hold one particular opinion rather than another, if he is to be saved. Christians may differ upon opinions and be saved by the same Father of our Lord Jesus Christ. Salvation is by personal relationship, not acceptance of doctrine.

> Hence, we cannot but infer, that there are ten thousand mistakes which may consist with real religion; with regard to which every candid, considerate man will think and let think. But there are some truths more important than others. It seems there are some which are of deep importance.... But surely there are some which it nearly concerns us to know, as having a close connection with vital religion.[11]

This same contention is well presented and convincingly made by Wesley in another sermon, "Catholic Spirit." Here he pleads for the reality of the experience, not for the different opinions by which they are doctrinally expressed. The major doctrines are presented and must be accepted, but the more nonessential and the more fully worked-out implications of the major doctrines are opinions and not mandatory to be held, if a man is to be saved.

> Persons may be quite right in their opinions, and yet have no religion at all; and, on the other hand, persons may be truly religious,

9. Ibid.

10. Wesley, *Journal*, 5:116.

11. Wesley, *Works*, 6:200.

who hold many wrong opinions. Can any one possibly doubt of this while there are Romanists in the world?[12]

And again, Wesley in his *Journal* urges the same typical approach.

> How little does God regard man's opinions! What a multitude of wrong opinions are embraced by all the members of the Church of Rome! Yet how highly favored have many of them been![13]

This one idea alone is backed by a multitude of references in the writings of Wesley. Quite obviously, one would wish that more of this had rubbed off on some of his followers, as well as other Christians. The wide acceptance of this idea alone would further the work of our ecumenical fellowship.

In his sermon "Catholic Spirit," Wesley attempts to give some basics that the Christian must believe in order to be Christian. He elsewhere is skeptical of listing those "fundamentals" necessary to be a Christian, and is aware of the dangers typically involved. However, he does give some important, central concepts of the Christian. Williams has gathered them thus:

> A review of Wesley's writings indicates that the essential doctrines on which he insisted included original sin, the deity of Christ, the atonement, justification by faith alone, the work of the Holy Spirit, and the Trinity.[14]

The points on which he insists before he gives his famous hand are: that one must have his heart right with God, believe in Christ, have his life of faith filled with love, do the will of God, serve God, love his neighbor, and show his love by works. It is only after asking these questions and getting an affirmative answer that Wesley gives his famous statement: " . . . then 'thy heart is right, as my heart is with thy heart.'"[15]

Wesley does not believe that the basic Christian doctrines are to be sacrificed, or sold for the pottage of an exaggerated show of brotherliness. There are doctrines of the utmost importance that must be presupposed and accepted before the opinions can even be discussed. The opinions do not matter in the order of salvation (i.e., qualify or disqualify one for salvation), but the doctrines are of a much higher importance.

12. Ibid., 6:199.

13. Wesley, *Journal*, 5:249.

14. Williams, *John Wesley's Theology Today*, 16–17.

15. Wesley, *Works*, 5:497–99.

In his sermon on the Trinity the same thing is said, Wesley does not care a whit how one would go about proving that there is a Trinity. He cares not how one imagines the three-in-one to be composed. He cares not how one thinks that the three operate. What he does care about is that we grant that there is a Trinity, a three-in-one. There is much to be said for this distinction between doctrine and opinion, which would be extremely helpful in our befuddled situation today.

To this point, we have found Wesley saying that persecution of the Roman Catholics is not worthy of Christian love. We have also found once more his emphasis upon the difference of doctrines (i.e., some are of major importance and some of minor), if you are to have fellowship with each other. Now, let us turn to the reception Wesley imagines the Catholics to receive from God.

Though certain that the Catholics are wrong in many of their opinions, yet he says they have received great favor of God. This fits in well with his refusal to write against those who have other *doctrinal opinions*, a belief he followed even stronger during the latter part of his life. The fact that the Romans were so highly favored by God was additional ammunition for his contention that opinions do not matter as much as many believed.

A large portion of common Roman Catholic-Protestant squabbles and differences fit Wesley's definition of "opinions." In a letter to a friend, Wesley writes:

> You have admirably well expressed what I mean by an opinion, contra-distinguished from an essential doctrine. Whatever is "compatible with love to Christ, and a work of grace," I term an opinion.[16]

Religion has little enough to do with opinions, for the essence of religion is not to be contained in doctrinal analysis. To Wesley, religion demands the relationship of a man with God and his fellow men. Opinions become worked out ideas of this vital and living relationship. Some men outstrip themselves in pressing for the opinions and not as hard for the essential doctrines. We could say that Wesley finds them guilty of majoring in minors. Wesley would have us not confuse fervor for opinions with fervor for Christianity.

> ... fervour for *opinions* is not Christian zeal. But how few are sensible for this! And how innumerable are the mischiefs which even

16. Ibid., 3:211.

this species of false meal has occasioned in the Christian world! How many thousand lives have been cast away by those who were zealous for the Romish opinions! How many of the excellent ones of the earth have been cut off by zealots, for the senseless opinion of transubstantiation![17]

We see that opinions based on a doctrine and the reality of the saving relationship with God may, and often do, differ. To Wesley, always the important point is the saving relationship between the person and God, not the rightness or wrongness of the opinion which the person has constructed in attempting to define the relationship and all of its ramifications.

In his sermon "Catholic Spirit," Wesley sketches in the rough outlines that all followers of Christ ought to believe. These beliefs are stressed before two Christians are to find their hearts the same and give to one another their hands. They are the basis of the unity that allows them to fellowship in this manner.

First, the person must have his heart or attitude right with God. This is taken to mean a saving knowledge of God. Involved in this process is God's being, perfection, eternity, immensity, wisdom, power, justice, mercy, and truth, among the other things. This is no small agreement for the person to make.

Second, the person is to believe in Christ. The prospective brother united in the belief that Christ is God, that He is the saving person, and that He has worked the miracle of salvation for the believer. It is well to note through the whole of these outlines that we are not speaking of opinions, but of foundations of the faith.

Third, one is to have his faith filled with love. The love of God is to be the proper content of the believer's heart. To love God with heart, soul, mind, and strength, and to love one's neighbor as oneself; this is the essence of the love about which Wesley is writing. He often refers us to Paul's thirteenth chapter of 1 Corinthians as the true love that we ought to have.

Fourth, the person is not to be a Quietist, but rather use his life in the stewardship of spending it following the will of God. The prospective brother must be a worker in the vineyard of God. He must not remain quiet and unemployed.

Fifth, service of God is to be rendered in fear or faith. The brother must reverence the God whom he serves.

17. Ibid., 7:64.

Sixth, a person must question the love that the brother has for all mankind. This love is to know no exception. Is the enemy loved? Is the enemy of God loved and served?

Seventh, one's love of God and neighbor is to be shown by works. While there is time in life and opportunity in space, service is to be rendered to the neighbor.

> Do you do them all the good you can; endeavoring to supply all their wants; assisting them both in body and soul, to the uttermost of your power?—If thou art thus minded, may every Christian say, yea, if thou art but sincerely desirous of it, and following on till thou attain, then "thy heart is right, as my heart is with thy heart."[18]

Notice that Wesley does not say that their hearts are together and in attune until all of these questions have been asked and the answers properly given. This is no easy acceptance of another, but properly grounded upon the realities of a common faith. Neither is it a minute examination of small opinions; rather it is an agreement on the basics of the Christian faith.

In a letter to his nephew Samuel Wesley, he writes about his fight with Rome, and the lack of his concern for opinions, but importance of the realities of religion.

> But meantime I have often been pained for you, fearing you did not set out the right way: I do not mean with regard to this or that set of opinions, Protestant or Roman (all these I trample underfoot), but with regard to those weightier matters, wherein, if they go wrong, either Protestants or Papists will perish everlastingly.[19]

It is only after we have properly focused our attention upon these former matters that we can fully appreciate Wesley's attack upon the failures of the Roman Catholic Church. We had first to make certain that we were not just enjoying a fight with Rome merely because it is habitual with Protestants. We had to see that Wesley is not just fighting because it was expected of him. He was one of the most lenient men of his day in his attitude towards the Roman Catholic Church, yet he found many failures evident in their religion. Both John M. Todd and J. Ernest Rattenbury have found this element in Wesley.

Among the biggest failures Wesley cannot abide is his charge that the Roman Catholics teach men to break the law of God and also that

18. Ibid., 5:499.
19. Wesley, *Letters*, 7:230.

they add to the Book of Life—the Bible. Some of the implications of this charge will be further worked out in this chapter. At this point, he is discussing the worship offered to or through images. To bow down before them, which Rome apparently advocates, is the essence of breaking the commandment of God not to worship images.

Wesley also finds some additions that Rome requires beyond that found in Scripture. Using the canons and decrees of the Council of Trent as his basis, Wesley charges them with the following additions:

1. Seven sacraments
2. Transubstantiation
3. Communion in one kind only
4. Purgatory, and praying for the dead therein
5. Praying to saints
6. Veneration of relics
7. Worship of images
8. Indulgences
9. The priority and universality of the Roman Church
10. The supremacy of the Bishop of Rome

All these things, therefore, do the Romanists add to those that are written in the Book of Life.[20]

The Romanists' high acceptance of the Mystics and their unscriptural doctrine is also something Wesley must stand against.[21] Preparing for his thrust against the doctrine of the Church as found in the Roman communion, Wesley begins by saying:

All the doctrines and practices wherein she differs from us were not instituted by Christ—they were unknown to the ancient Church of Christ—they are unscriptural, novel corruptions; neither is that Church "propagated throughout the world."[22]

As to the church itself, Wesley charges that it is not one, holy, or sealed against error. As far as being one, Wesley says that "it is not in unity with itself; it is to this day torn with numberless divisions."[23] The Roman Church is and always has been divided. He points out that other parts such as the Asiatic, African, and Russian Catholics were never within the Roman Catholic Church.

20. Wesley, *Journal*, 2:264.
21. Wesley, *Letters*, 5:313.
22. Wesley, *Journal*, 4:436.
23. Ibid.

As far as being holy, "The generality of its members are no holier than Turks or Heathens."[24] Wesley's proof is to look at the innumerable Catholics he met and talked with on his trips throughout the whole country. In his discussions with them he finds that they are not holy.

As far as being sealed from error, one can almost hear the biting words, "witness Pope against Pope, Council against Council, contradicting, anathematizing each other."[25]

After reading a book about the lives of the Mystic saints, Wesley is sure that they lived highly improbable lives, their "virtues" were not really virtues at all, and the actions they performed not laudable. Not only this, but to clinch the argument, he finds them full of enthusiasm—in its bad sense.[26] For example, Wesley railed against enthusiasts who sought the ends of religion without using the means. That is, they bypassed the Church and the offer of grace that God had given. The enthusiasts of Wesley's day were against the Church and the ordinances of the Church and claimed to possess the Holy Spirit without using the means of grace given by God to this Church. To Wesley this was very wrong.

Let us now turn to Wesley's thoughts about the misconceptions the Roman Catholic Church has concerning its ministry.

The succession of pastors and teachers that Rome teaches is a point that can be used to the Protestant advantage, in either of two ways. If we think of the succession of pastors as those who are divinely appointed and divinely assisted to perform their calling, both the Romans and the Protestants have always had them. The chief means by which Wesley would have their appointment by God tested is to see if they have been able to bring in converts. Pastors and teachers in both the Church of Rome and the Protestant communions must successfully pass this test.

> This Church has "a perpetual succession of pastors and teachers divinely appointed and divinely assisted." And there has never been wanting in the Reformed Churches such a succession of pastors and teachers, men both divinely appointed and divinely assisted; for they convert sinners to God—a work none can do unless God Himself doth appoint them thereto and assist them therein . . .[27]

24. Ibid.
25. Ibid., 4:437.
26. Ibid., 4:540.
27. Wesley, *Letters*, 4:137.

If, however, we wish to place our whole emphasis upon the uninterrupted succession of pastors and teachers, we find that there is no such thing upon the face of the earth. For the church to declare that there are no ministers outside of the communion of this succession, whose work has the authority of the apostles handed down to them, is to lose the Romans as well as the Protestants.

> I deny that the Romish bishops came down *uninterrupted* succession from the Apostles. I never could see it proved; and I am persuaded I never shall. But unless this is proved, your own pastors on your principles are no pastors at all.[28]

So we find that either way one would wish to understand succession, the Protestant ministry is on as sound a basis as the Roman, if not better founded by some interpretations. If we suppose that the uninterrupted succession is mandatory for the Roman Catholic priesthood, then the Protestant ministers stand on better ground than the Romans. This is so, for they do not make this demand upon their ministers and Wesley cannot find conclusive evidence for the Roman contention.

The conclusion of the matter Williams rightly points out, is that a breaking point must come at times between the visible community, the continuity of the Word, and mission of the Church. When this point comes, we are to stick with the continuity of the Word and the mission of the Church.[29] When looked at in this light, the Protestant ministry stands firm.

Wesley is never convinced that there is an uninterrupted succession of bishops from Rome.[30] Likewise, things such as the wealth of the Pope,[31] gave rise to the possibility of calling the Pope a "son of perdition."[32] By way of explanation, the Popes were involved in secular affairs in the fourteenth century and were among the wealthiest men alive. They also lost a great deal of credibility during what is now called the "Great Schism." This occurred after the Papacy moved back to Rome and the Cardinals elected Urban VI. Urban was more dictatorial that they liked so they nullified their choice and elected Clement VII. Urban didn't like this so he excommunicated Clement

---

28. Wesley, *Letters*, 4:140.
29. Williams, *John Wesley's Theology Today*, 229.
30. Wesley, *Notes*, 581.
31. Ibid., 403.
32. Ibid., 766.

and Clement returned the favor by excommunicating Urban. Charging each other with heresy brings ridicule upon their heads.[33]

Another addition is that the Roman Catholics raise the Pope above the status that Wesley will allow. The Pope finds no preeminence in his thought; the Catholic idea of Peter's receiving the authority from Christ and his passing it down from bishop to bishop, is a fable that Wesley will not believe. The point of his attack comes in the Romans making a distinction between Peter and the other disciples.

> But that he gave one Apostle pre-eminence above the rest, much less absolute power over them, we read not. This power they were forbidden to attempt or desire; (Matt 20:26) and St. Paul was so far from acknowledging it, that he challenged an equality with the rest of the Apostles, (Gal 1:15–17) and, upon occasion, withstood St. Peter (Gal 2:11).[34]

Not only was this true, but when Christ is speaking of the "rock," He is speaking of the faith of Peter and not Peter himself. "On this rock—alluding to his name which signifies a rock: namely the faith which thou hast now professed."[35]

The final failure that we will discuss in this section is the Roman theology of the sacraments. Agreeing with the Protestant tradition, Wesley maintains the existence of only two sacraments instituted and commanded by Christ. The others believed in by the Roman Church are not true sacraments, in the same sense of the word. He finds that Peter Lombard around 1139 AD defined the number of the sacraments, and that St. Austin is positive that there are only two divinely instituted sacraments. With a crushing finality, and as a true son of the Reformation, Wesley writes in his "Roman Catechism, and Reply":

> Now, that there should be sacraments of divine institution, that are neither instituted in the gospel, nor known to be so till 1100 years after our Saviour, nor be made a matter of faith till 1500, may be a doctrine received in the Church of Rome, but will not easily be believed by any out of it.[36]

---

33. Wesley, *Letters*, 1:277–78.

34. Wesley, *Works*, 10:88.

35. Wesley, *Notes*, 81.

36. Wesley, *Works*, 10:113.

In the following hymn, Wesley attacks many of the Roman misuses of the sacraments. This hymn places emphasis upon the one sacrifice by Christ on the cross, once given, as opposed to the Roman doctrine of the sacrifice of the Mass. It also points out that no work of man is capable of earning our salvation, thereby emphasizing that justification is by faith alone.

> All hail, Thou mighty to atone!
> To expiate sin is Thine alone,
>   Thou hast alone the wine-press trod,
> Thou only hast for sinners died,
> By one oblation satisfied
>   Th' inexorably righteous God.
>
> We only can *accept* the grace,
> And humbly our Redeemer praise,
>   Who bought the glorious liberty;
> The life Thou didst for all procure
> We make, by our believing, sure
>   To us who live and die to Thee.[37]

To summarize the failures of Roman Catholicism, we see throughout that Wesley charges them with salvation by faith *and* works. The problem with their interpretation is that they place works as coequal with faith in the order of salvation—not that works are unimportant to the individual Christian, but they do not count toward salvation. They instead are a result flowing from our accepting God's grace of salvation (i.e. good works follow, not precede, salvation). To the Roman Catholic, faith and works combine to give one salvation. A man has responsibility for works before he is saved and salvation is, in part, based upon works. To Wesley, works are important; but they offer nothing for salvation. Faith is the single basis. Works grow out of faith; they are faith's fruits.

> That faith which hath not works, which doth not produce both inward and outward holiness, which does not stamp the whole image of God on the heart, and purify us as He is pure; that faith which does not produce the whole of the religion described in the foregoing chapters, is not the faith of the gospel, not the Christian faith, not the faith which leads to glory.[38]

---

37. Rattenbury, *Eucharistic Hymns*, 236.
38. Wesley, *Standard Sermons*, 2:33–34.

Wesley is close to the Roman Catholic emphasis upon the value of works for the Christian. In fact Wesley was often accused of being a Roman Catholic himself. His emphasis on works continues to be evident in his followers today. However, Wesley puts works on the other side of justification. Works follow justification in the order of salvation. In and of themselves, they have no merit attached to them. As we have seen, the Romans place tradition above Scripture in such things as having seven sacraments instead of the two that Wesley finds to be scriptural. It is also interesting to note that the two sacraments are actually in accord with the tradition of most of the church's history. Wesley likewise finds their priesthood not as well established as the Protestant, for upon their own foundations they fail. According to Roman Catholic belief, the priest, when consecrating the sacraments, must have an intention of doing at least what the church does and intends for him to do, likewise the Pope, etc. If the priest is of another mind or is not consciously intending well in the consecration of the sacraments—if his mind wanders, he thinks of other things, he is thinking ill of other people—there is a real question whether the sacraments have any value to the recipient. Should the Pope not intend well, all priests ordained by him deliver sacraments of no value. Wesley finds problems with an uninterrupted priesthood and charges this whole system with many corruptions. We find him thus urging the three great Reformation and Protestant doctrines: justification by faith, Scripture as the foundation of Christianity, and the priesthood of all believers. Though we have not time to run down each of these, they are at the bottom of the whole discussion. *Wesley's Hymns* gives abundant evidence in the section entitled "Salvation by Grace."

Further discussion of the failures will come in the comparison of Roman Catholicism with True Christianity, or True Religion, as Wesley believed and taught it. He compiled many of the errors into a workable outline that we will discuss later.

ROMAN CATHOLICISM AND SALVATION

On this topic Wesley is once more strangely silent. However, with a few of his statements we can make many inferences why this is so, and the basis of what we believe to be his position. There is an interesting statement in his *Journal* in which he talks about the fact that he is widely thought of as a Catholic. He tells of writing a letter to a Roman Catholic priest as follows: "No Romanist, as such, can expect to be saved, according to the terms of the Christian covenant."[39]

This statement leaves open many possibilities of salvation for the Catholics. One would have to define too much to make this an absolute in the case of every Catholic. We would have to know what Wesley meant when he said, "as such." If he meant a Catholic as a Catholic, then we have no worry, for no Methodist as a Methodist or Baptist as a Baptist ought to expect salvation from this fact alone, though some Christians seem to think it true. If, on the other hand, he meant no Catholic who is a good Catholic and follower of the doctrines could be saved, we have something quite different.

Because of the ambiguity of this statement, and the clarity of other statements in which he allows the possibility of Romanists to be saved, I think we can properly maintain that he here is not meaning to exclude all Catholics from salvation.

In a letter to John Newton, he defends the possibility of salvation for the Roman.

> Is not a Papist a child of God? Is Thomas à Kempis, Mr. De Renty, Gregory Lopez gone to hell? Believe it who can. Yet still of such (though Papists) the same is my brother and sister and mother.[40]

I think Wesley rarely thought of this as a problem and only writes in provocation from those who would seek to exclude the Romans from the possibility of fellowship and salvation through Christ. Because these potential problems are not mentioned enough in his writings we can conclude that they were of little concern for him.

The clearest statement the writer has found in Wesley is in his sermon "On Faith," in which he discusses the various levels of human faith.

> ... the faith of the Roman Catholics, in general, seems to be above that of the ancient Jews. If most of these are volunteers in faith, believing more than God has revealed, it cannot be denied that they believe all which God has revealed, as necessary to salvation. In this we rejoice on their behalf: We are glad that none of those new Articles, which they added, at the Council of Trent, "to the faith once delivered to the saints," does so materially contradict any of the ancient Articles, as to render them of no effect.[41]

39. Wesley, *Journal*, 5:296.
40. Wesley, *Letters*, 4:293.
41. Wesley, *Works*, 7:198.

Here we have a clear statement that the Romans have the necessary ingredients for saving faith. They make additions, to be sure, but they have all that is necessary. It is well for us today to ponder these things and attack in brotherly love those things we consider additions, but keep as brothers those who hold to them.

Again Wesley writes:

> But we cannot doubt, that many of them, (Roman Catholics) like the excellent Archbishop of Cambray, still retain (notwithstanding many mistakes) that faith that worketh by love. And how many of the Protestants enjoy this, whether members of the Church of England, or of other congregations?[42]

It seems highly likely from what we have discussed that it hardly entered Wesley's head to dismiss a Roman Catholic from salvation just because of his church affiliation. There are mistakes, additions, and opinions that he considered dead wrong and he found other problems with Catholicism to be sure, but through it all he believed many of them to have the essentials of the saving faith. They may make too many things essential, but still the real essentials of True Christianity are present and undoubtedly will be sufficient for the salvation of many.

I think the scarcity of Wesleyan statements upon the point of salvation for the Roman Catholic points more to an open acceptance of them than a considering of them outside the possibility of salvation. Surely, he scarcely considered that they would be excluded for their Catholicism.

As to the famous distinction between Roman Catholics and Protestants on the doctrine of Justification, Wesley is very lenient. While he certainly believes in justification by grace alone through faith alone, he holds open the possibility of being justified by faith, even when the person is attempting to fulfill the Roman Catholic doctrine of faith and works. Though they express their doctrine wrongly, they will be saved by faith—trusting the God known through Christ for this salvation.

> The human righteousness of Christ, at least the imputation of it, as the whole and sole meritorious cause of the justification of a sinner before God, is likewise denied by the members of the Church of Rome; by all of them who are true to the principles of their own Church. But undoubtedly there are many among them whose experience goes beyond their principles; who, though they are far

42. Ibid., 7:201.

from expressing themselves justly, yet feel what they know not how to express. Yea, although their conceptions of this great truth be as crude as their expressions, yet with their hearts they believe: They rest on Christ alone, both unto present and eternal salvation.[43]

It is fitting to close this section with a quote written about Wesley by a twentieth-century Roman Catholic:

> In the end, he regarded the traditional Christian doctrines as final: there was no question of "Turks" or any others having a religion which might offer a proper basis, comparable with Christianity, or some syncretic religion. But Wesley worked on the basis that a man may sincerely want to work for God, and indeed be able to work for him, without having the full truth; his whole life and teaching is based on "the one thing necessary" and he carries this out to its logical conclusion in all spheres.[44]

ROMAN CATHOLICISM AND "TRUE CHRISTIANITY"

Possibly the best way to make a comparison between Roman Catholicism and True Christianity, is to follow Wesley through his "A Roman Catechism," to see what he has to say about it. In this catechism Wesley follows a consistent pattern of comparison that is helpful to our study.

Wesley is always the protagonist for True Religion, therefore the comments offered here are important in our comparison between Roman Catholicism and True Religion or True Christianity. In matters of fact, they summarize what is scattered throughout the *Works*, *Letters*, and *Journal*. He divided the area into four major heads: The Church and Rule of Faith, Repentance of Obedience, Divine Worship, and the Sacraments.

First, as to the church, Wesley cannot allow the Pope the power that his church would confer upon him. We discussed this earlier and found that Peter was not given preeminence over the other apostles. "Indeed, not to him alone (for they were equally given to all the apostles at the same time, John 20:21–23), but to him were first given the keys both of doctrine and discipline."[45] As to the Church of Rome being the mother of the churches, he shows that Jerusalem has the nod here, for she was the first

---

43. Ibid., 5:242.
44. Todd, *Wesley and the Catholic Church*, 98.
45. Wesley, *Notes*, 81.

mother. Even if it be contended that Rome ought to be so designated because she was an imperial city, he finds Constantinople was one as well.

> Ye different sects, who all declare,
> "Lo here is Christ." or, "Christ is there!"
> Your stronger proofs divinely give,
> And show me where the Christians live.
>
> Your claim, alas! Ye cannot prove;
> Ye want the genuine mark of love:
> Thou only Lord, thine own canst show;
> For sure thou hast a church below.[46]

The preeminence of the Roman Church above the others is not found in her authority. The gospel was preached and received by St. Paul, not from others, particularly not others from the church at Rome, but by a revelation of Christ to him. In point of fact, St. Paul had very little to do with the church in Rome. The anathema, which he placed upon those who preach another gospel, squarely hits the Roman Church in their bowing before images. The Scripture argues with the Roman contention of this authority.

The additions that the Roman Church makes to the faith once given, comes under the attack of Wesley. Placing his foundation squarely upon the Scriptures, he says:

> For as all faith is founded upon divine authority, so there is now no divine authority but the Scriptures; and, therefore, no one can make that to be of divine authority which is not contained in them. And if transubstantiation and purgatory, etc., are not delivered in Scripture, they cannot be doctrines of faith.[47]

Wesley continues his attack by pointing out the fundamental nature of the Scriptures for Christianity. The Scripture is the supreme authority, for it is the divine spokesman to the Church, as interpreted through the Holy Spirit. The Church is not the supreme authority, rather it stands upon the authority of the Scriptures, and in turn, is judged by it.

> . . . as long as we have the Scripture, the Church is to be referred to the Scripture, and not the Scripture to the Church; and that as the Scripture is the best expounder of itself, so the best way to

---

46. Wesley, *Wesley's Hymns*, no. 16, vv. 6–7.
47. Wesley, *Works*, 10:91.

know whether anything be of divine authority, is to apply ourselves to Scripture.[48]

Second, in the section upon repentance and obedience, Wesley covers
works, indulgences, purgatory, and limbo. This whole area revolves around
the discussion of repentance and the meanings found therein. The doctrine
of penance is at the base of the whole Roman defection, and its divergence
from True Religion, at this point. After explaining contrition as a sorrow for
past sin, and a desire not to commit it again, which needs penance to receive
forgiveness; and explaining attrition as an imperfect contrition needing
confession, Wesley slices the heart out of the Roman contention.

> The same texts which make contrition sufficient, without con-
> fession to the Priest, make attrition insufficient without there
> be contrition. And as the former doctrine of the insufficiency of
> contrition without confession, makes that necessary which God
> hath not made necessary; so this latter of the sufficiency of attri-
> tion upon confession to the Priest without contrition, makes that
> unnecessary which God hath made necessary.[49]

This double defection signals to Wesley the complete collapse of the
Roman doctrine of penance. The whole structure built upon the foundation of penance must collapse if this blow at its roots is successful. "Are
not the sins of one who truly repents, and unfeigned believes in Christ,
remitted without sacerdotal absolution; and are not the sins of one who
does not repent or believe *retained* even with it?"[50] Wesley contends that
this is an improper foundation that allows the whole system of doctrine
to be built upon it. The whole system of doctrine falls because it has been
built upon an improper foundation. These doctrines seem destined for a
theological limbo, as they have no basis upon which to stand. A typically
Wesleyan answer would be to say that he could not believe them while he
believed his Bible.

Third, is the section that covers divine worship. Here the main arguments arise out of a concern for the language to be used in worship, the
objects of worship, and the pretense given for worshipping such objects.

The language matter is simply disposed of by Wesley. In worship we
are to first attend to the end or goal, and then we are to use the best means

48. Ibid., 10:94.

49. Ibid., 10:95.

50. Wesley, *Notes*, 387.

possible for that end. The end of worship is to glorify God and to edify the Church of God. This makes possible a definition of the means to that end. The means for worship is to have services that inform the mind, stimulate the emotions, and increase devotion: "But that cannot be done, where the tongue it is celebrated in is not understood."[51]

There is no need to work through each of the objects of worship that Wesley discusses (i.e., angels, saints, Mary, memorials, relics, images and pictures, and the crucifix). An interesting anecdote might help us here. Wesley met a Roman Catholic woman who had broken her china crucifix and was in agony of mind, telling her priest, "Oh, sir, what must I do? I have broken my china crucifix, and now have nothing to trust to but the great God of heaven."[52] To this exclaimed Wesley, "What a mercy, what a mercy that this poor woman had at length nothing to trust to but the great God of heaven."[53] It is enough for us to get to the bottom of the matter as quickly as possible. Thus Wesley pursues the same thought throughout the whole section. For his attack, Wesley quotes Jesus, "Thou shalt worship the Lord thy God, and him only shalt thou serve." From this point he continues:

> As divine worship is due to God, as it is not lawful to give it to any other. The Church of Rome doth acknowledge this, but says the worship they give to saints and angels is not of that kind. . . . But what worship is peculiar to God, if prayer is not? So thought St. Ambrose: "Thou only art to be invocated." For God alone can receive our prayer, or can give what we pray for, or be the object of our faith and trust.[54]

It is enough for one to apply this thought to each of the objects of worship of the Roman Catholic, to find adequate materials to fight their doctrines.

As to what pretense is offered which allows them to reverence such things, the Romans say they represent not God, but some of the qualities or properties of God. Wesley's reply is twofold. The first is: How does this answer those representatives that you make which have no scriptural

---

51. Wesley, *Works*, 10:102.
52. Wesley, *Journal*, 8:79.
53. Ibid.
54. Wesley, *Works*, 10:103.

basis? The second is: God never appeared in any forms whatsoever, how then can images be accepted? And,

> . . . God cannot be represented at all, but by such properties and effects; but if an image of God be forbidden to be worshipped, then the image, even by such properties and effects, is forbidden to be worshipped.[55]

The fourth and final section of the "Roman Catechism and Reply," concerns the sacraments. Wesley gets in an anticipatory blow early in his definition of a sacrament by speaking of the parts of the sacrament, as the Catholics define them. Catholics urge a distinction between "matter" and "form," but Wesley does not find this distinction to be consistent.

> That a sacrament should consist of matter and form, and yet either have no form, as confirmation and extreme unction; or have neither matter nor form, of divine institution, as penance and matrimony, is to make them sacraments, and to be none. Our Church rightly affirms of the additional sacraments, they have not any visible sign ordained of God.[56]

Wesley urges this concept throughout the remainder of his discussion of the Roman sacraments. There is no need for us to bog down in a discussion of the minor abuses of the sacraments when we have found the whole basis of the extra sacraments to be entirely without foundation, even the foundation upon which the Romanists themselves urge. They "have partly grown out of the *corrupt* following of the apostles, and partly are states of life allowed in the Scriptures, but yet have not the like nature of Baptism and the Lord's Supper, because they have not any visible sign or ceremony ordained of God."[57]

Wesley brilliantly catches the inconsistency in question fifty-eight of the Roman Catechism where it says that God must institute all sacraments,[58] yet one of the great schoolmen says that Christ did not institute confirmation to be a sacrament. Fast exegetical footwork must be engaged in to get one out of such a position as this.

Wesley objects to the Roman contention of *ex opere operato* (from the work done) that the virtue of the sacraments comes from the per-

55. Ibid., 10:112.

56. Ibid., 10:113.

57. *Book of Discipline*, 63.

58. Wesley, *Works*, 10:116.

formance of the sacrament rather than the holiness or worthiness of the priest. He contends that the virtue of the sacraments does not come from the mere performance of the rite, but from the blessing involved in the relationship with God.[59]

> Settle this in your heart, that the *opus operatum*, the mere *work done*, profited nothing; that there is no *power* to save, but in the Spirit of God, no *merit*, but in the blood of Christ; that, consequently, even what God ordains, conveys no grace to the soul, if you trust not in Him alone . . . he that does truly trust in Him, cannot fall short of the grace of God, even though he were cut off from every outward ordinance, though he were shut up in the centre of the earth.
>
> Remember also, to use all means, *as means*; as ordained, not for their own sake, but in order to the renewal of your soul in righteousness and true holiness. If, therefore, they actually tend to this, well; but if not, they are dung and dross.[60]

Thus we find the work of God within the person, in fulfilling His promises, is the important event within the sacrament—not just the performance of the outer form.[61] This point is well illustrated by one of the Wesley hymns on the Lord's Supper.

> Let the wisest mortal show
>   How we the grace receive,
> Feeble elements bestow
>   A power not theirs to give.
> Who explains the wondrous way,
>   How through these the virtue come"
> These the virtue did convey,
>   Yet still remain the same.
>
> Sure and real is the grace,
>   The manner be unknown;
> Only meet us in Thy ways,
>   And perfect us in one.
> Let us taste the heavenly powers;
>   Lord, we ask for nothing more;
> Thine to bless, 'tis only ours
>   To wonder and adore.[62]

59. Ibid., 5:201.
60. Ibid., 5:201.
61. Ibik., 10:113.
62. Rattenbury, *Eucharistic Hymns*, 213.

His objection to the belief that the priest is vital to the validity of the sacraments is that such a contention uncovers nothing but problems.

> . . . if there be no intention, the sacraments are none. And so there is no certainty whether the Priest be a Priest, or whether in the eucharist the elements continue not elements after consecration, and what is taken for the host be no other than bread. For without the intention, neither is the Priest ordained, nor are the elements consecrated.[63]

In answer to the Roman doctrine of transubstantiation of the elements in the Mass, whereby there is a conversion of the bread and wine into the substance of Christ's body and blood, Wesley urges three points.

First, from the Scriptures themselves there is no need to infer a change of substance from the bread to the body of Christ. It "cannot be proved by Holy Writ, but is repugnant to the plain words of Scripture, overthroweth the nature of a sacrament, and hath given occasion to many superstitions."[64] Cardinal Cajetan acknowledges that there is no change in the substance of the symbols, and places the source of the doctrine upon the tradition and authority of the Church.[65]

Second, the words found in the Scriptures concerning the consecration of the elements (1 Cor 10:17; 11:26–28), are not to be taken in their usual meaning. There is no radical conversion as the Romans contend to be found in the Scripture, because that which is called His body is likewise called bread at the same time.

> The body of Christ is given, taken, and eaten in the Supper, only after a heavenly and spiritual manner. And the means whereby the body of Christ is received and eaten in the Supper is faith.[66]

Third, the mystical relation of Christ's body to the consecrated bread is enough to merit it being called the body of Christ:

> For it is the usual way of Scripture, to call things of a sacramental nature, by the names of those things they are the figures of. . . . So, circumcision is called the covenant . . . [67]

63. Wesley, *Works*, 10:114.
64. *Book of Discipline*, 64.
65. Wesley, *Works*, 10:118.
66. *Book of Discipline*, 64.
67. Wesley, *Works*, 10:118.

This is enough to give us a taste of the great divergences Wesley finds between the Roman aberrations and True Christianity. True enough the two are both founded upon Christ as Lord and Savior. However, the Roman Church has a penchant for additions to the things that are necessary for salvation. Some of these additions have been hurtful to the members of that communion. The additions may help lead the followers astray from the central doctrines of the Christian faith and the most meaningful matters of the Christian life.

Not only are there additions that are hurtful, but there are glaring inconsistencies and downright falsehoods propagated by Rome. The only way in which they have been continued is to remove the foundation of the church from the single one of God as revealed in the Scripture, and add the second foundation of tradition. To place tradition equal, if not at times greater, in importance than the Scriptures is to open the door to all the mistakes for which Rome contends. We must, therefore, stand firmly upon the single basis of the God revealed in the Christ of our Scriptures, as interpreted to us through the means of the Holy Spirit.

So we find Roman Catholicism to be Christian, however unusual and unique they have made themselves. Their falsehoods are to be fought, but the individual is to be accepted as a brother in the faith, given through our common Lord and Savior, Jesus Christ.

Beware how you attempt to hinder him, either by your authority, or arguments, or persuasions. Do not in any wise strive to prevent his using all the power which God has given him. If you have *authority* with him, do not use that authority to stop the work of God. Do not furnish him with *reasons* why he ought not any more to speak in the name of Jesus.[68]

As a closing thought, we might point out that a good deal has been written concerning the relation of John Wesley to the Roman Catholic Church. Despite the attacks found in his writings, there are many points at which Wesley comes close to the doctrinal affirmations of Catholicism. Were it not true, one such as John Todd, of the Roman communion, could not write a book like *John Wesley and the Catholic Church*. However unconvincing this book may be in many of its points—the author seems to be stretching or bending Wesley too far to make his point—nonetheless, the mere fact the book exists is important.

---

68. Wesley, *Standard Sermons*, 2:118, 115–16.

Rattenbury points out this nearness in the doctrine of love. The typically Protestant emphasis he finds to be upon faith, and the typically Catholic emphasis upon love. Rattenbury places Wesley in the center, between these two extremes, describing his position as a faith working by love.

> . . . the emphasis of the love of God and the neighbor as the total requirement of the Christian life in its highest ranges and deepest experiences is perhaps more reminiscent of the Catholic than the Protestant devotion. It reminds one more of Francis of Assisi or of Francis de Sales than of Martin Luther, Ulrich Zwingli, John Calvin, or John Knox. He restored love to its Pauline place in Protestant theology. "The greatest of these is love."[69]

This is an oversimplification of the distinctions between the Roman Catholic and Protestant, to be sure. It does point out Wesley's emphasis upon love. He is not alone in this either. A major book such as Bishop Anders Nygren's *Agape and Eros*, shows the Protestant emphasis on love to be of major importance.

Wesley was plagued over the years by his opponents unfairly calling him a Roman Catholic and a Papist.[70] Again and again this is evident in his letters and journals. He cannot understand why he is so taken and misunderstood, but possibly this is a partial answer. One cannot doubt the emphasis upon love, which is found in this poem:

> O grant that nothing in my soul
>   May dwell but Thy pure love alone!
> O may Thy love possess me whole,
>   My joy, my treasure, and my crown!
> Strange flames far from my heart remove,
> My every act, word, thought, be love![71]

Though one cannot doubt the emphasis upon love in Christianity as well as in this poem, surely we would not want to contend that all emphasis on love is strictly a Catholic one. Surely, we must uphold the thesis of Nygren in *Agape and Eros* that Luther once more brings agape back into the prominence that it ought to have.

Lee, quoting George Cell, says that Wesley united the Protestant ethics of grace and the Catholic ethics of holiness. "This is a wise and a just

69. Rattenbury, *Wesley's Legacy*, 168–69.

70. Wesley, *Journal*, 2:262–63, 3:46–47, 8:305; *Letters*, 3:295–331.

71. Wesley, *Journal*, 5:117.

observation. Holiness comes to man by the indwelling of the Holy Spirit, and man receives the Spirit by faith."[72] Again, an oversimplification, but it illustrates a point. Wesley does stand in the great tradition between Roman Catholicism and Protestantism, with the Anglican Church. This undoubtedly has consequences in the doctrinal interpretations that he makes.

He even makes distinctions when he says that the things believed by people "will supply the absence of love." He lists them in this order: "talking well," "knowledge," "faith," "good works," and finally, "suffering for righteousness' sake." "Nothing is higher than this, but Christian love; the love of our neighbour, flowing from the love of God."[73]

Likewise, his emphasis upon the importance of the more essentials as opposed to the opinions of Christianity might get him a bit close to Rome in some people's minds. However, he was thoroughly opposed to the additions to Christianity that Rome made, so this contention does not carry an abundance of merit. Wesley had no trouble in signing a declaration against Popery.[74]

Cannon finds Wesley closer to Rome on the doctrine of sanctification than justification, which seems to be natural. Luther broke with Rome on justification and the Protestants have pushed it, whereas growth in grace and emphasis upon God's love in sanctification was all too often lost.[75]

Sugden compliments Wesley on his good feeling for the Roman Catholics and the realistic appraisal of them.

> He enumerates the essential points on which Protestants and Romanists are agreed, and pleads that on this basis they should work together in brotherly love and sympathy. But he came to see later the hopelessness of expecting any fraternal feeling or co-operation from the Romanists . . .[76]

It would be hard to imagine how a man could allow more freedom of opinion and at the same time more staunchly maintain his own convictions, than Wesley does in his writings concerning the Church of Rome.

Nothing could be more fitting than to close this section with Wesley's poem on Catholic spirit, as Franz Hildebrandt has collected them:

72. Lee, *Wesley and Modern Religion*, 190.

73. Wesley, *Works*, 7:51.

74. Wesley, *Journal*, 3:125.

75. Cannon, *Theology of John Wesley*, 245.

76. Wesley, *Standard Sermons*, 2:115–16.

Ye different sects, who all declare,
Lo, here is Christ, and Christ is there,
Your stronger proofs divinely give,
And show me where the Christians live![77]

One family we dwell in Him,
  One Church, above, beneath,
Though now divided by the stream,
  The narrow stream of death:
One army of the living God,
  To His command we bow;
Part of His host have crossed the flood,
  And part are crossing now.[78]

---

77. Hildebrandt, *Christianity According to the Wesleys*, 73; Wesley, *Wesley's Hymns*, no. 16.

78. Hildebrandt, *Christianity According to the Wesleys*, 79.

6

Quakerism and "True Christianity"

IT IS EXCEEDINGLY DIFFICULT to get hold of Wesley's thought on the problem of Quakers and True Christianity because there is little writing in which he explicitly takes up the Quakers, and less still in which he deals with them directly on our point. He was sure that they failed in being fully Christian; perhaps that is the best way for us to begin.

THE QUAKER FAILURE

In his letter to Thomas Whitehead, later printed As "A Letter to a Quaker," Wesley lists the differences he finds between Quakerism and Christianity. The grand failure of the whole movement is that they have fallen from the high calling to which they were called. They have fallen from a meaningful religion to one full of *opinions*. They have allowed their religion to become one of majoring in minors. This fall is basic to each of the separate failures he lists.

> You was zealous once for the love of God and man, for holiness of heart and holiness of life; you are now zealous for particular forms of speaking, for a set of phrases and opinions. Once your soul was against ungodliness and unrighteousness, against evil tempers and evil works; now it is against forms of prayer, against singing psalms or hymns, against appointing times of praying or preaching; against saying "you" to a single person, uncovering your head, or having too many buttons upon your coat.[1]

Quakerism's fall from True Christianity was into the trap of letting *opinions* become the basic doctrines of the faith, and thereby letting the more basic doctrines slip into the background of preaching and the life of the Church. Throughout this book, we have seen Wesley debate this same

1. Wesley, *Letters*, 2:127.

point with others. Nowhere does he do it more explicitly and effectively than in his disagreements with the Quakers.

The first failure Wesley lists concerns the Quaker use of the Scriptures. Quakers allow both private revelations and the Scripture to be valid guides for the Christian life. Wesley thinks that they allow the private revelations too much validity. They do grant that private revelations are not to contradict right reason or Scripture, but will not really examine private revelation from a scriptural basis.

Against this point of view Wesley contends, "the Scriptures are the touchstone whereby Christians examine all, real or supposed revelation."[2] In every case of revelation versus Scripture, the Christian is to appeal "'to the law and to the testimony,' and try every spirit thereby."[3] Instead of so judging, the Quakers seem to keep them separate, in airtight compartments. They allow the validity of Scripture over experience, but in practice do not make the application. For Wesley, the Scriptures are the basic of the Christian life. It is through them that God speaks. God interprets God, for us to understand, in our study of God's Word.[4]

Wesley is likewise afraid that by placing the validity of Christianity upon revelations rather than the Scripture the Quakers will be lead in the wrong direction. With the Quaker, Wesley is in agreement that the Holy Spirit is the principal ground of truth and faith. However, if we do not continuously test these spirits and revelations by the Scripture, to determine whether they are the Holy Spirit or another, we leave ourselves open for all sorts of errors. "For though the Spirit is our principal leader, yet He is not our rule at all: the Scriptures are the rule whereby He leads us into all truth.[5]

Williams well and adequately summarizes Wesley's purpose and point at this juncture of our discussion.[6] The basis of Wesley's thought is to be found from two *Standard Sermons*, "The Witness of the Spirit," and "The Witness of our Spirit." Wesley begins the former with these words:

> How many have mistaken the voice of their own imagination for
> this witness of the Spirit of God, and thence idly presumed they

2. Ibid., 117.

3. Ibid.

4. Wesley, *Wesley's Hymns*, no. 255, vv. 1–3.

5. Wesley, *Letters*, 2:117.

6. Williams, *John Wesley's Theology Today*, 108–12.

> were the children of God, while they were doing the works of the
> devil! But with what difficulty are they convinced thereof, espe-
> cially if they have drank deep into that spirit of error! All endeav-
> ors to bring them to the knowledge of themselves, they will then
> account fighting against God; and that vehemence and impetuos-
> ity of Spirit, which they call "contending earnestly for the faith,"
> sets them so far above all the usual methods of conviction, that we
> may well say, "With men it is impossible."[7]

Williams has excellently distilled the two main points that Wesley
makes. The first is that the testimony of God's Sprit must come before
the testimony of our spirit. "The Christian is aware of being grasped
by God's Spirit, an awareness which, of course, may bring about feeling
reactions, but is self-authenticating and not explicable in terms of sense
experience."[8]

Williams has secondly found that Wesley points to *objective* marks
by which we may be able to distinguish true from false assurances. These
objective marks are: repentance, awareness of a great change within the
life, fruit of the Spirit, and newness of outward life.

> The reason why Wesley pointed to these scriptural tests for dis-
> tinguishing true from false assurance lies in his conviction that by
> the Spirit at work within us a faith relationship to Christ is certain
> to be followed by those inward and outward changes of which the
> tests speak.[9]

This is enough evidence to point out the fear that Wesley had of
those he considered in danger of placing more importance upon the experiences of life, or private revelations, than upon the Scripture.

The next failure with which Wesley charges them is that they do not
touch the scriptural doctrine of justification by faith. Their doctrines and
practices lead to justification by works, instead. Having himself been caught
in this theological trap in his younger days, Wesley is aware of the difficulties involved. Justification is a gift of God's grace, not a work of man.

> The things that were not, His mercy bids live;
> His mercy unbought We freely receive;
> His gracious compassion We thankfully prove,
> And all our salvation Ascribe to his love.[10]

---

7. Wesley, *Works*, 5:111–12.

8. Williams, *John Wesley's Theology Today*, 110.

9. Ibid., 111.

10. Wesley, *Wesley's Hymns*, no. 212, v. 5.

Wesley leaps into the controversy with his sermon "The Lord our Righteousness." In this sermon he wages a war on many fronts, one of which is that against the Quakers. The Quaker denial of the imputation of Christ's righteousness means that they stand upon the doctrine of justification by works. They rely not upon the merits of Christ applied to their spirit, but upon the works they are able to accomplish in this life. Wesley quotes Robert Barclay, the Quaker author:

> As many as receive the light, in them is produced an holy and spiritual birth, bringing forth holiness, righteousness, purity and all other blessed fruits. By which holy birth, as we are sanctified, we are justified.[11]

This doctrine Wesley takes to be a complete inversion of the Christian faith. It is a complete turning of the whole, upside down, "whereas the Christian doctrine is, that 'we are justified by faith.'"[12] The works of Christ are given by grace to a sinner who responds to the work of God in Christ. Therefore it is given not for the sake of works, but "unto him that worketh not, but believeth on Him that justifieth the ungodly, his faith is counted to him for righteousness."[13]

Against this perversion of the Christian faith, Wesley quotes a hymn that more correctly states the matter:

> While thus we bestow
> Our moments below,
> Ourselves we forsake,
> And refuge in Jesus's righteousness take.
> His passion alone,
> The foundation we own;
> And pardon we claim,
> And eternal redemption in Jesus's name.[14]

Now, lest some say that Wesley has just involved himself in a controversy over words, we show that he is not concerned for the particular expression used to present the religious reality. Regardless of how it is expressed, he desires that the Christian experience of the righteousness of

11. Wesley, *Letters*, 2:118.

12. Ibid.

13. Ibid.

14. Wesley, *Works*, 5:242.

Christ being applied to our spirits be a reality of the person's experience. It would be hard to prove him wrong here.

The Quakers are but one of the long list of contenders that Wesley charges and then seems to partially clear of this mistake. He first charges them with the theological mistake, but clears some of them by saying undoubtedly many of them had the reality of the experience, but not the ability to verbally describe it. He quotes James Hervey as "Words, worthy to be wrote in letters of gold":

> We are not solicitous as to any particular set of phrases. Only let men be humbled as repenting criminals at Christ's feet, let them rely as devoted petitioners on his merits, and they are undoubtedly in the way to a blessed immortality.[15]

The next failure Wesley finds in the Quakers is a peculiar one to bring up in our day of female ministers in The United Methodist Church. He charges Barclay with making a difference between Quakerism and Christianity because the Quakers allow women to preach in the assemblies. Between the two men there is a skirmish of scriptural exegesis, in which Wesley seems to come out with a better biblical interpretation. However, the ministry that some women render to the Church of God today makes it a bit uncomfortable for one to rigidly follow Wesley's line of thought at this point. God seems to have learned quite a bit over the years and found that women are as capable as men in preaching the Word of God and leading their churches.

In matters of worship, Wesley finds various differences of importance, which we ought to consider seriously. Wesley charged the Quaker attitude of waiting until the Spirit moved them to speak as being based upon an incorrect interpretation of Scripture. Being "moved by His Spirit," means the reason of man, as well as his emotions. The speaker need not wait until the Spirit strokes his emotion, man's reason could be quickened as well.

> God moves man, whom He has made a reasonable creature, according to the reason which He has given him. He moves him by his understanding as well as his affections, by light as well as by heat. He moves him to do this or that by conviction full as often as by desire. Accordingly you are as really "moved by the Sprit" when He convinces you you ought to feed him that is hungry, as when He gives you ever so strong an impulse, desire, or inclination so to do.[16]

15. Ibid., 5:243.

16. Wesley, *Letters*, 2:120.

Here is strong reasoning power added to good exegetical work. The Quakers are not wrong in going as far as they have gone; they just have not completed the matter.

To wait for the emotional touching of man by God's Spirit is to greatly limit the working power of the Spirit within the life of man. Were men not rationally convinced by the Scripture and God's Word, as well as emotionally moved by it, we would be vastly impoverished from our present condition. The Spirit of God may work in the study and long range planning, as well as upon the spur of the emotional moment.

Turning the tables on Barclay, Wesley charges him and the Quakers with "will-worship," a pejorative term in the extreme to the Quakers. Their silence, with no words or actions "in the natural will and comprehension, and falling after the inward seed of life,"[17] is gross "will-worship." Wesley can find no example of it within the scriptures; neither does he find a command for it.

The real worship of God is quite different from the teachings of the Quakers. The worship of God is "whatever is said or done in the sight or love of God, that is full of spirit and life."[18] Everything else is the form in which the worship appears. The importance is the reality, not the form of worship. If this is true, and certainly it is, then the Quakers have been vastly wrong in placing their emphasis upon the form and not the spirit of worship.

Wesley next assails the Quaker position of not using the sacraments. In his sermon "The Means of Grace," Wesley defines the means as:

> By "means of grace" I understand outward signs, words, or actions, ordained of God, and appointed for this end, to be the ordinary channels whereby he might convey to men, preventing, justifying, or sanctifying grace.[19]

The different means described by Wesley are prayer, Scripture, and the Lord's Supper.[20] Following this lead, in "A Treatise on Baptism," Wesley defines baptism as:

> What it is. It is the initiatory sacrament, which enters us into covenant with God. It was instituted by Christ, who alone has power

17. Ibid., 2:123.
18. Wesley, *Works*, 8:189.
19. Ibid., 5:187.
20. Ibid., 5:188.

to institute a proper sacrament, a sign, seal, pledge, and means of grace, perpetually obligatory on all Christians. We know not, indeed, the exact time of its institution; but we know it was long before our Lord's ascension. And it was instituted in the room of circumcision. For, as that was a sign and seal of God's covenant, so is this.[21]

This definition points out the necessity of the sacrament of baptism for the grace which God gives through this means. Using a couple of quotes from Wesley, Sugden also points to the importance of the sacraments.[22]

In answer to the next question as to whether baptism was meant to continue through the centuries of the Christian Church, Wesley answers unequivocally "yes." Just as circumcision was the means of grace and entry into the Jewish covenant, so baptism is the means of grace and entry into the Christian covenant. "By plain parity of reason, baptism which came in its room, must last among Christians as long as the gospel covenant into which it admits, and whereunto it obliges, all nations."[23]

Against this position, Barclay argues that the Lord's Supper has ceased to have the substance that is figured by the bread and wine. Wesley agrees to many of Barclay's points, but that the Lord's Supper has lost its substance, he denies. Barclay backs his interpretation by contending that the Lord has already returned in the form of the Holy Spirit, and therefore he finds no need for the continuing of the supper. Since Christ has come to the believer and lives within the form of the Spirit, there is no need to keep this outer form of the sacrament, which merely pledges the reality that men already know.

Wesley devastates this argument by first showing that St. Paul had nothing whatsoever to do with it. St. Paul wrote to the Corinthians to continue their performance of the Lord's Supper until Christ comes. If it were just until the spiritual return of Christ in the form of the Holy Spirit within the spirit of man, surely some of the communicants at that time were filled with this Spirit. According to the Quaker way of thinking, Paul would not have found it necessary to ask them to partake of the elements. But, Paul commands them so to do. "It remains, that he speaks of His coming in the clouds to judge both the quick and the dead."[24] The

21. Ibid., 10:188.
22. Wesley, Standard Sermons, 1:240.
23. Wesley, Works, 10:192.
24. Wesley, Letters, 2:125.

Quakers have again blown up their own case by a misinterpretation of the Scriptures.

The reality of the sacraments and their meaningfulness to the community of Christ is to be found in the Articles of Religion, which Wesley revised and sent over to the American Methodists:

> Sacraments ordained of Christ are not only badges or tokens of Christian men's profession, but rather they are certain signs of grace, and God's good will toward us, by which he doth work invisibly in us, and doth not only quicken, but also strengthen and confirm, our faith in him.[25]

The sacraments are to be understood as real and important means of grace for the Christian. They have been instituted by Christ and are a gift of God's grace to His children.

A hymn, possibly written by John Wesley, but if not, written by his brother under joint commendation, shows the importance that he places upon the Lord's Supper for the Christian.

> With joy we feel its sacred power,
> But neither stars nor means adore;
> We take the blessing from above,
> And praise the God of truth and love.
>
> What he did for our use ordain
> Shall still from age to age remain;
> Whoe'er rejects the kind command,
> The word of God shall never stand.[26]

Thus, the great divergences between Christianity and Quakerism have been covered in these objections. As Sugden comments, "he (Wesley) objected to Quakerism, because it set aside ordination and the sacraments, and taught that all worship other than that to which a man is directly moved by the Spirit is abominable idolatry [parentheses mine]."[27] Wesley's objections are all scriptural in that they involve the teaching of the Scriptures and the interpretation of these Scriptures. Wesley sums up

---

25. *Book of Discipline*, 63.

26. Rattenbury, *Eucharistic Hymns*, no. 62, vv. 8–9.

27. Wesley, *Standard Sermons*, 1:240.

the greatest of these differences "In what Robert Barclay teaches concerning the Scriptures, Justification, Baptism, and the Lord's Supper."[28]

The next differences are not as important as these four preceding, however, they are important enough for Wesley to point them out to Thomas Whitehead in "A Letter to a Person Lately Joined with the People Called Quakers."[29]

Wesley calls the Quaker refusal to accept titles of honor a totally unnecessary scruple. The Quakers, following Barclay, sought to solve one of the sharpest objections raised against them by fast shuffling of exegetical interpretation of a passage in which Paul calls the Roman Governor, "Most Noble." Barclay attempts to prove that the man is a good man and therefore worthy of the title that Paul bestows upon him. Wesley's answer is to prove by Scripture that the Governor was not an honorable man, which is the damaging blow to Barclay.

Wesley attacks the use of "thee" and "thou" by the Quakers as an idle scruple in which they mistake the scriptural meaning of plain language. Plain language Wesley interprets to mean not this form of usage, but "he . . . who . . . uses the plain language who speaks the truth from his heart."[30] He allows them the liberty of this usage, but denies their correctness of scriptural interpretation.

> I do not desire you to refrain from saying *thou* or *thee*. I would not spend ten words about it. But I desire you, whenever you speak at all, to speak the truth, and nothing but the truth. I desire your words may always be the picture of your heart. This is truly plain language.[31]

Swearing before a magistrate is another of the differences between Quakerism and Christianity found by Wesley. In this onslaught, Wesley has his man backed against the wall. He crushes the argument of Barclay by pointing to a case in which Jesus Himself answered upon an oath before a magistrate.[32]

The whole disagreement between the Quakers and Christianity is that the Quakers put too much weight upon the smaller points of the law.

28. Wesley, *Letters*, 2:125.
29. Ibid., 2:116–28.
30. Ibid., 2:126.
31. Wesley, *Works*, 8:185.
32. Wesley, *Letters*, 2:126.

They give little weight to the more important things and matters. If they change their point of view, they would be much better. If they change their point of view, if they return to scriptural Christianity and the sacraments that God has given, they would be much closer to the more important issues and True Christianity.

> Come back, come back to the weightier matters of the law, to spiritual, rational, scriptural religion. No longer waste your time and strength in beating the air, in vain controversies and strife of words; but bend your whole soul to the growing in grace and in the knowledge of our Lord Jesus Christ, to the continually advancing in that holiness without which you cannot see the Lord.[33]

QUAKERISM AND SALVATION

However confused and confusing the doctrines of these men may be, Wesley was not willing simply to consign them all to hell. He was willing, and rightly so, to say that their doctrines might be greatly in error, but they might have the reality of religion, which is salvation.

Wesley presents the need for the sacrament in a hymn.[34] Baptism is the washing away of original sin, and being brought into the Christian community. Wesley allows that there are those who do not know the more precise and exact definition of the doctrine, but who may have the experience itself. Though the outer sign be absent, the grace of God may be a reality in the life of such a person. While mightily contending for the sacrament of baptism, he admits that the grace of God is not entirely bound within the sacrament.

> You think the mode of baptism is "necessary to salvation": I deny that even baptism itself is so; if it were, every Quaker must be damned, which I can in no wise believe. I hold nothing to be (strictly speaking) necessary to salvation but to the mind which was in Christ.[35]

Further triumph of this way of thinking is found in the discussion about the imputed righteousness of Christ. Though the Quakers know nothing of the righteousness of Christ being imputed to their spirits, this

33. Ibid., 2:127–28.
34. Wesley, *Wesley's Hymns,* no. 476.
35. Wesley, *Letters,* 3:36.

does not make impossible the reality of Christ's imputation. Though the doctrine be entirely absent, the Spirit can be, and often is, present.

> But will any one dare to affirm that all . . . Quakers . . . who are not clear in their opinions or expressions, are void of all Christian experience?—that, consequently, they are all in a state of damnation, "without hope, without God in the world?" However confused their ideas may be, however improper their language, may there not be many of them whose heart is right toward God, and who effectively know "the Lord our righteousness?"[36]

This point concerns the imputed righteousness of Christ, or salvation. Justification is the end point of this discussion. Wesley makes possible justification and therefore salvation for those who have not the doctrine, but have the reality of the religious experience.

Wesley's love and esteem for the Quakers is evident in various comments that he makes through his works. His *Journal* gives to us the circumstances of his running across the journal of William Edmundson, a Quaker preacher. He was highly impressed by the journal's presentation of the man and his life. If he could believe the account, which he seems to have done, he thought exceedingly high of the man. However, he was not willing to subscribe to his doctrine, though he considered his life to be that of a good Christian.

> His opinions I leave; but what a spirit was here! What faith, love, gentleness, long-suffering! Could mistake send such a man as this to hell? Not so. I am so far from believing this that I scruple not to say, "Let my soul be with the soul of William Edmundson!"[37]

Here seems account enough to impress us with the acceptance Wesley greeted the Quakers who he thought have a saving relationship with God. At least, he did not consider it an impossibility for them, even though he found them greatly lacking and in error in their theological formulations.

Time and again we have seen how Wesley will deny the opinions and doctrines of those with whom he disagrees, but we have also seen that he allows each of them their Christian experience. They may make vast mistakes in the scriptural interpretation of their experiences, but if the reality of the experience with God be present, Wesley will "give his hand,"

---

36. Wesley, *Works*, 5:243.
37. Wesley, *Journal*, 5:137.

in fellowship. It is not that Wesley is unconcerned with either doctrines or opinions; he has both and fights for them. But, he is not willing that differences of opinion separate him from those who, having the same God, had the same inner experience. The dynamic, saving relationship with God is given priority always over formulation of the Christian faith.

For Wesley, the reality of the relationship of a man with God is far more vital than man's interpretation of this relationship. He places an exceedingly high value upon the construction of doctrine and opinion, but he will not let this separate him from presenting to the world a united front with them. This fight of opinions is to be carried on within the boundaries of the church. From the position of one outside the church, all they are to see is a united front around the basic doctrines of the faith. Surely, these are ideas for modern Methodists and the ecumenical movement to ponder.

QUAKERISM AND "TRUE CHRISTIANITY"

The differences between True Christianity and Quakerism are important for us to consider. Though these differences are not the kinds which have the power of determining heaven and hell for the adherent of them, they are important for us to recognize in order to understand Wesley and the True Christianity that he spread throughout much of the English speaking world.

Wesley is, at all times, an exponent of True Christianity. From the beginning of his search for salvation to his death, this is his foundation. His statements about Quakerism should largely be understood as deriving from this position. Each of the failures Wesley finds in Quakerism comes from this point of view. An understanding of this will help us interpret Wesley's approach to each of the differing points of view he considers.

The use of Scripture by the Quakers is not fully productive of the fruits of True Christianity. Fruits there might be, but not the fruits Wesley desired from his study of the Scriptures. Throughout his whole life, Wesley was addicted to the Scripture. His interpretation of Christianity strictly was based upon them, with the added dimension of human reason. From this foundation he stood against all who would make serious battle in a realistic manner. Those who missed the point so far that the time and trouble would be more than the gain, Wesley always dismissed.

By allowing private revelations to supersede the Scriptures at certain points, Wesley found the Quakers in danger of moving too far from the basic foundation of Christianity. To be sure, this is not so much in their theory as it is found in their practice. They are in danger of wandering from the scriptural foundation of Christ. True Christianity is based upon the Scriptures, and the belief that all that is necessary to salvation is contained within them.

> The Holy Scriptures containeth all things necessary to salvation; so that whatsoever is not read therein, nor may be proved thereby, is not to be required of any man that it should be believed as an article of faith, or be thought requisite or necessary to salvation.[38]

One may well return to the preface to the *Standard Sermons*, to remind himself of the Wesleyan emphasis upon the Scriptures. The "man of one book" is a man who bases his sermons as well as life itself, upon the revelation of God within the Scriptures. The man who wants sermons as void of Scripture and theology as possible would not be able to stand the sermons written by Wesley. He is unashamedly founded upon the Scriptures and makes his theology come from the study of them with the added dimension of reason.

> I have accordingly set down in the following sermons what I find in the Bible concerning the way to heaven; with a view to distinguish this way of God from all those which are the inventions of man. I have endeavoured to describe the true, the scriptural, experimental religion, so as to omit nothing which is a real part thereof, and to add nothing thereto which is not.[39]

The grand scriptural doctrine of justification by faith is the foundation of the Wesleyan revival. It is this doctrine, when rightly preached, that brought the fathers of the Church of England down upon his head. It is this doctrine, when rightly preached, that released the miners and laborers from their sins and led them into a life of holiness, pursuing the goal of sanctification and eternal life. His denial of the way of works finds vent in his early sermon "Salvation by Faith," and is a continuing emphasis throughout his life.

---

38. *Book of Discipline*, 62.
39. Wesley, *Works*, 5:4.

... "If a man cannot be saved by all that he can do, this will drive men to despair." True, to despair of being saved by their own works, their own merits, or righteousness. And so it ought; for none can trust in the merits of Christ, till he has utterly renounced his own.[40]

Wesley's own definition of Christianity makes void any attempt of man to justify himself with works of holiness.

Christian faith is then, not only an assent to the whole gospel of Christ, but also a full reliance on the blood of Christ; a trust in the merits of his life, death, and resurrection; a recumbency upon him as our atonement and our life, *as given for us*, and *living in us*; and, in consequence hereof, a closing with him, and cleaving to him, as our "wisdom, righteousness, sanctification, and redemption," or, in one word, our salvation.[41]

From this basis we can understand Wesley's point against the Quakers. His own early life, in which he sought justification by works, taught him a lesson that he never forgot and one that he sought to help others learn. From *Wesley's Hymns* of 1876, we find a good statement of the Wesleyan position on faith and works.

Plead we thus for faith alone,
Faith by which our works is shown:
God it is who Justifies;
Only faith the grace applies;
Active faith that lives within,
Conquers earth, and hell and sin,
Sanctifies, and makes us whole,
Forms the Savior in the soul.

Let us for this faith contend,
Sure salvation is its end:
Heaven is already begun,
Everlasting life is won.
Only let us persevere,
Till we see our Lord appear,
Never from the rock remove,
Saved by faith, which works by love.[42]

---

40. Ibid., 5:14.
41. Ibid., 5:9.
42. Wesley, *Wesley's Hymns*, no. 521, vv. 3–4.

We can also see why Wesley is able to allow so much room for variance of thought to those who differed with him. He can point to the reality of the experience for which he is contending, and allow those who disagree with him the possibility of having the experience. However, they from their point of view seldom allow the same room for him. If he contends for the experience, it may truly be a reality, even if one doctrinally constructs the experience differently. However, if one contends for the doctrine, that person can hardly allow experience that differs from him or those who find doctrinally different expressions.

Differences in worship may be handled in a similar manner. Wesley is continually contending for the reality of the religious experience, and others often contend for the outer manifestation of the religions experience. Wesley can allow outer changes of form and still contend for the spirit of the inner experience. However, those who contend for the outer conditions of worship and not the inner experience cannot allow to him the lenience that he allows to them. This well could be a word to our day of ecumenical endeavors.

> I say, all religion is either empty show, or perfection by inspiration; in other words, the obedient love of God, by the supernatural knowledge of God; Yea, all that which "is not of faith is sin;" all which does not spring from this loving knowledge of God; which knowledge cannot begin or subsist one moment without immediate inspiration; not only all public worship, and all private prayer, but every thought in common life, and word, and works.[43]

In like manner, he can allow the Quakers the possibility of salvation, even though they do not have the sacraments of baptism or the Lord's Supper. He does not minimize the importance of the sacraments, for he believes them to be instituted by Christ. He finds God's grace through the sacraments and perceives that man receives many benefits from partaking of them. He fights with them on this point, but he does not allow this to make impossible the saving experience and relationship with God.

Wesley says they make the mistake of believing no means are valuable because a few great men of their number received God's grace without using the normal means.[44] Wesley thinks the Quakers have again placed emphasis upon the end of religion, to the exclusion of the means

43. Wesley, *Works*, 8:188.
44. Ibid., 5:187.

that God has provided. The means can be of no value unless the goal is kept in mind;[45] yet, the goal is ordinarily given only by faithful attendance upon the means.[46]

True Christianity believes and uses all of the means of grace because the basic experiences and relationships of True Christianity can best be found within them. However, this is not to deny the possibility of the experience occurring outside of these means. The means are best from the scriptural and rational point of view, but the relationship with God is possible outside the use of these particular means. The True Christian, of whom Wesley speaks, sees God in His ordinances. "Whether they search the oracles of God, or hear the ambassadors of Christ proclaiming glad tidings of salvation; or by eating of that bread, and drinking of that cup, in all these His appointed ways, they find such a near approach as cannot be expressed. They see Him, as it were, face to face."[47] The means are God-given and man is meant to use them.

> According to this, according to the decision of holy writ, all who desire the grace of God are to wait for it in the means which he hath ordained; in using, not in laying them aside.[48]

> Settle this in your heart, that the *opus operatum*, the mere *work done*, profiteth nothing; that there is no *power* to save but in the Spirit of God, *no merit*, but in the blood of Christ; that, consequently, even what God ordains, conveys no grace to the soul, if you trust not in Him alone. On the other hand, he that does truly trust in Him, cannot fall short of the grace of God, even though he were cut off from every outward ordinance, though he were shut up in the centre of the earth. . . . Remember also, to use all means, *as means*; as ordained, not for their own sake, but in order to the renewal of your soul in righteousness and true holiness. If, therefore, they actually tend to this, well; but if not, they are dung and dross.[49]

True Christianity seeks always a unity of witness to the world, but maintains the fight for the opinions it embraces, within the ranks of the

45. Ibid., 5:188.
46. Wesley, *Standard Sermons*, 1:421.
47. Ibid., 1:361.
48. Wesley, *Works*, 5:190.
49. Ibid., 5:201.

total Christian Church. True Christianity pleads that we all show our oneness in Christ to the world and fight out among ourselves our differences of opinion within the Christian ranks.

> Wesley's great concern was for unity in witness. But this did not mean that he considered the points of difference of no importance. Instead, he believed that when the task moved from witness to the world to nurture of the faithful, some of these differences were of very great importance.[50]

Wesley deplored the vast differences between True Christianity and Quakerism. He fights against it as effective as he possibly can. Yet, he can find no valid reason for excluding them from God's grace.

Wesley speaks words of wisdom to our age in which the forms of religion have outstripped the reality of our relationship with God. Then again what age can say it has truly effectively remained innocent of this?

---

50. Williams, *John Wesley's Theology Today*, 18.

7

Mysticism and "True Christianity"

WE NOW DISCUSS THE relation between Mysticism and True Christianity. Mysticism has always been a pleasure and yet a plague to Christianity. In its more acceptable forms, it has fostered some of the greatest leaders of the Church. However, in some of its extremes, these great Christians are so extreme that few dare to follow, much less teach others to follow in the same paths.

DEFINITION OF MYSTICISM

In order to make our definition of Mysticism as clear as possible, let us begin with a modern definition and then work back to the Mysticism in Wesley's day. William James has defined Mysticism by emphasizing four major elements, which he finds in all types and forms of Mysticism. The Mystical experience, according to James, is *ineffable*; it is outside the categories of description. The experience of the Mystic is deeply personal and cannot wholly be described to another. The experience defies the categories of normal expression and conversation.

The Mystical experience also has a *poetic* quality. When one is actually plunged into the experience, he feels himself able to penetrate deep into unplumbed truths. Truths seem to be found and realized which can be found in no other way.

It is *transient*. The Mystical condition or experience cannot be held for long periods of time. The experience is outside the boundaries of our full control, no matter how hard we seek to rule it.

The Mystic feels the Mystical experience in such manner that he becomes *passive*. The experience is not directed by the Mystic, but is enjoyed by him. The events of the experience are not under the Mystic's control. In this manner James defines Mysticism.[1] Now, let us think about the days in which Wesley lived. During the period of the Commonwealth, there were many Mystical groups to be found within England. Lee thinks they were primarily seeking "to save a belief in the immediate communion of man with God."[2] This is one point at which Wesley was afraid that the Mystics were too extreme.[3]

This was no unimportant controversy in which Wesley found himself. The times were unusual. Fanaticism seemed rampant, especially in the more humble (poor, uneducated) families of England. Conditions were so extreme that:

> The claim to immediate inspiration, what was called "enthusiasm," was no unimportant matter in the seventeenth century; and philosophers, theologians, and statesmen joined to combat the pretensions of those who asserted a revelation from God Himself.[4]

Lee finds four live, available options for the religious person of Wesley's day, giving us a little of the religious flavor of the period. First was *rationalism*, which spoke for a minimum amount of belief and universal acceptance of what was held to be true by all men. The people worked for a universal religion, acceptable to all. Next was *corporate religion*, with its emphasis upon the church and the organizations that are a part of all organized church life. Third, some, and especially the Quakers, emphasized the *religion of the inner life*. Finally, there were some *prophetic* and *Mystical* groups with their advocates.[5]

One of the major difficulties in discussing Wesley and Mysticism is that we must first discover which type of Mysticism is under consideration. Mysticism is widely varied; indeed, Wesley himself says that there are about as many forms of Mysticism as there are people calling themselves Mystics.

> There are excellent things in most of the Mystic writers. As almost all of them lived in the Romish Church, they were lights whom the gracious providence of God raised up to shine in a dark place. But they do not give a clear, a steady, or an uniform light. That wise

1. James, *Varieties of Religious Experience*, 414–15.
2. Lee, *Wesley and Modern Religion*, 36.
3. Wesley, *Journal*, 1:420.
4. Lee, *Wesley and Modern Religion*, 37.
5. Ibid., 38.

and good man Professor Franke used to say of them, "They do not describe our *common Christianity*, but every one has a religion of *his own*." It is very true: so that if you study the Mystic writers, you will find as many religions as books; and for this plain reason, each of them makes his own experience the standard of religion.[6]

James caught this very thing: "I imagine that these experiences (Mystic) can be as infinitely varied as are the idiosyncrasies of individuals [parentheses mine]."[7]

McConnell points to only one aspect of Mysticism with which Wesley was dealing. The single feature of Mysticism that he describes is "that which puts stress on reaching for ends without means."[8] This he finds to correspond with Wesley's definition of enthusiasm, and certainly this is one factor Wesley has in mind with his discussions with the Mystics.

This concept of McConnell's, however, falls short of the mark. Wesley not only discusses the Mystics from this point of view, but he attacks them in their acceptance of private revelations and the unscriptural speculations that arise from them as well.

Lee only finds the first group of Mystics, for he writes:

> By the mystics, of whom he later spoke with unusual harshness, Wesley meant apparently the Quietists, who taught that man must wait quietly and passively without moral striving or institutional helps for the moving of the Spirit of God.[9]

This is a major thrust of Wesley's argument with the Mystic writers, but he did argue with them on other points as well.

An early letter Wesley wrote to his brother Samuel shows the same concern with those who seek the end in religion without using the means God has given for it.

> I think the rock on which I had the nearest made shipwreck of the faith, was, the writings of the Mystics; under which term I comprehend all, and only those, who slight any of the means of grace ... [10]

---

6. Wesley, *Letters*, 6:43–44.

7. James, *Varieties of Religious Experience*, 445.

8. McConnell, *John Wesley*, 158.

9. Lee, *Wesley and Modern Religion*, 69.

10. Wesley, *Works*, 12:27.

In summarizing his findings against Mystics, Wesley writes from the Mystic perspective:

> All means are not necessarily for all men; therefore each person must use such means, and such only, as he finds necessary for him. But since we can never attain our end by being wedded to the same means; therefore, we must not obstinately cleave unto anything, lest it become a hindrance, not a help.[11]

Wesley applies this measuring stick to public prayer, Scripture, the Lord's Supper, and Christian perfection. This is enough to point out the sort of Mystics Wesley had in mind.

THE MYSTIC FAILURE

The Mystic failure may largely be summed up by once more saying that followers seek the end of religion without using the means God has provided for man. They seek communion and union with God to such an extent that they do not use the means God has given for this purpose. As we have seen, the means of public prayer, Scripture, the Lord's Supper, and Christian perfection are all involved in the dispute.

This failure is once more attacked in Wesley's sermon, "The Nature of Enthusiasm."

> A third very common sort of enthusiasm . . . is that of those who think to attain the end without using the means, by the immediate power of God. If, indeed, those means were providentially withheld, they would not fall under this charge. . . . But they who expect this when they have those means, and will not use them, are proper enthusiasts. Such are they who expect to understand the holy Scriptures, without reading them, and meditating thereon; yea, without using all such helps as are in their power, and may probably conduce to that end. Such are they who designedly speak in the public assembly without any premeditation. I say "designedly"; because there may be such circumstances as, at some times, make it unavoidable. But whoever despises that great means of speaking profitably is so far an enthusiast.[12]

11. Ibid.
12. Wesley, *Standard Sermons*, 2:99.

Some of the Wesleyan hymns speak boldly against the mistake of the Mystics in pursuing the goal of religion without using the means God has given.

> Still, for by loving-kindness, Lord,
>   I in thy temple wait;
> I look to find thee in thy word,
>   Or at thy table meet.
>
> Here, in thy appointed ways,
>   I wait to find thy will:
> Silent, I stand before thy face,
>   And hear thee say, "Be Still!"[13]

Certainly this covers the field of those who seek the end of religion without using the means to that end. They are guilty not because it is impossible to find God without using them, rather they are guilty because God has offered them and the means are not being withheld from them.

Wesley finds them guilty of denying the gifts that God has given to us. In a letter to Ann Bolton, Wesley states that they deny these gifts, and further " . . . make a kind of merit of it; to imagine we honor Him by undervaluing what He has done."[14] To applaud the denial of that which God has offered to mankind is indeed to place one in a peculiar position, especially if one is seeking to be a Christian.

Another example of religious ends without means is the Mystic emphasis upon periods of darkness in the development of the spiritual life. They are to stand by "naked faith," faith without support of or without experiencing the presence of God, when all else seems to slip away. This condition is thought first to be higher than continuous living in the light of God's love, and responding with love, peace, and joy.[15]

> The Scripture nowhere says that the absence of God best perfects His work in the heart! Rather, His presence and a clear communion with the Father and the Son: a strong consciousness of this will do more in an hour, than His absence in an age. Joy in the Holy Ghost will far more effectually purify the soul, than the want of that joy; and the peace of God is the best means of refining the soul from the dross of earthly affections. Away then with the idle conceit,

13. Wesley, *Wesley's Hymns,* no. 92, vv. 1–2.
14. Wesley, *Letters,* 5:313.
15. Wesley, *Standard Sermons,* 2:253.

that the kingdom of God is divided against itself; that the peace of God, and joy in the Holy Ghost, are obstructive of righteousness; and that we are saved, not by faith, but by unbelief; not by hope, but by despair![16]

Christianity, Wesley teaches, is more often a slow growth in the grace of God, by using all the means God has made available, than it is a swift growth in union with God without the means of grace. The efforts of man in using the means of grace are not works of salvation; they do not save because of their performance. However, if one makes himself available to receive the grace which God has graciously provided, he may receive salvation as a gift. The essence of enthusiasm is to seek the end or goal of the means without using the means that God has given.

> Beware . . . of imagining you shall obtain the end without using the means conducive to it. God can give the end without any means at all; but you have no reason to think He will. Therefore constantly and carefully use all those means which He has appointed to be the ordinary channels of His grace. Use every means which either reason or Scripture recommends, as conductive (through the free love of God in Christ) either to the obtaining or increasing any of the gifts of God.[17]

The short-circuiting of the means in order to quickly arrive at the ends led many of the Mystics into Quietism. After all, to what does the non use of the means lead but Quietism?[18] This is what Wesley charged the well-known French Mystic Madam Guyon with doing. In a letter to Miss Mary Bishop of Keynsham he says:

> Madam Guyon was a good woman, and is a fine writer, but very far from judicious. Her writings will lead any one who is fond of them, into unscriptural Quietism. They strike at the root, and tend to make us rest contented without either faith or works.[19]

This is the second of Wesley's double-headed attack upon the Mystics. He is sure that God's grace is abundant and will be given to all those who seek after it. All of God's good gifts are given to those who are willing to rouse their spiritual energies in the effort of seeking, in order to find.

16. Ibid., 2:261–62.
17. Ibid., 2:103.
18. McConnell, *John Wesley*, 150.
19. Wesley, *Works*, 13:25.

Quietism, or the resting content with seeking the end of Christianity without the God-given means, leads to yet another of the Mystic failures. These followers fail to recognize the communal aspect of Christianity. Their emphasis is so heavily placed upon the individual and what the individual is experiencing or not experiencing, that they forget we are to be in community. They are so busy taking their individual experience temperatures they forget that Christianity is a community. We have seen that Wesley has charged them with having as many religions as they have interpreters of the Mystic way, which is an end product of their extreme individualism.

Wesley shows us the connection between the fallacy of Quietism and the fallacy of individual religion in his sermon "Upon our Lord's Sermon on the Mount: IV." After first showing that many urge us to follow the way of Quietness, he speaks of the Master's message to us:

> Here he defends, in the clearest and strongest manner, the active, patient religion He had just described. What can be fuller and plainer than the words He immediately subjoins to what He had said of doing and suffering " . . . In order fully to explain and enforce these important words, I shall endeavor to show, first, that Christianity is essentially a social religion; and that to turn it into a solitary one is to destroy it."[20]

He finds it difficult to believe that one can read the Scriptures and remain a Quietist. The direct commands of Christ ran counter to any such belief, for those commands cannot be fulfilled if one remains apart from society, apart from other Christians.

> For that the religion described by our Lord in the foregoing words cannot subsist without society, without our living and conversing with other men, in manifest from hence, that several of the most essential branches thereof can have no place if we have no intercourse with the world.[21]

Not only do the Mystics slight the company of others in the practical working out of their religion with their neighbor, but they depart from the institutional framework of their religion. Wesley charges them with having no conception of church fellowship. "The chief of them do not appear to me

20. Wesley, *Standard Sermons*, 1:381–82.
21. Ibid., 1:382.

to have any conception of church communion. Again, they slight not only works of piety, the ordinances of God, but even works of mercy."[22]

The Mystics are continually calling us to go apart, to leave the society of men and refresh our souls in the presence only of God. Wesley admits that there is value in such an approach, but does not allow that this is the whole sum and completeness of Christianity. Some of the most important elements of Christianity are found only when the community of Christ becomes a reality. The Mystics speak of going apart to receive God's grace.

> Whereas, according to the judgment of our Lord, and the writings of his Apostles, it is only when we are knit together that we "have nourishment from Him, and increase with the increase of God" ... The gospel of Christ knows of no religion, but social; no holiness but social holiness. "Faith working by love" is the length and breadth and depth and height of Christian perfection.[23]

Solitary religion is not the religion of Christ. Christianity must exist in community if it is to be the religion taught by Christ. The hymns of John and especially Charles Wesley also echo this point. *Wesley's Hymns* of 1880, numbers 515–522, all place some emphasis upon it. For example:

> While we walk with God in light,
> God our hearts doth still unite;
> Dearest fellowship we prove,
> Fellowship in Jesu's love:
> Swiftly each, with each combined,
> In the bonds of duty join'd,
> Feels the cleansing blood applied,
> Daily feels that Christ hath died.[24]

So strongly does Rattenbury feel this conflict between the solitary religion of the Mystics, and the institutional religion as taught by Wesley and the main line of the Church, he writes:

> The real competitor with mysticism is Institutional Religion. The lesson Wesley learnt as a young man—that he could not go to heaven without companions—was one of the deepest realities of

---

22. Wesley, *Works*, 3:160.
23. Ibid., 14:320–21.
24. Wesley, *Wesley's Hymns*, no. 522, v. 2.

his life. Now mysticism could not flourish in a social community; but love could flourish there, real love.[25]

This is undoubtedly partly true, but one may doubt whether it should be pushed to the extreme, which Rattenbury does, for there are other questions involved in this discussion between Wesley and the Mystics. Certainly the greatest distinction between Mysticism and True Christianity is the point that Mystics seek ends without the means, which often leads to Quietism, which in turn leads to a separation from the institutional structure of Christianity.

> Against the hermetic ideal of the mystics, however, he held that human fellowship was an attribute of holiness; and against Quietist mysticism he maintained that love of our neighbor was inseparable from love to God. Love must be expressed in actions.[26]

The impossibility of being Christian and living exclusively apart from the fellowship of other Christians is strongly felt even in the Wesleyan hymns and the area of "fellowship" found in the index.

> All praise to our redeeming Lord,
>   Who joins us by his grace,
> And bids us, each to each restored,
>   Together seek his face.
>
> He bids us build each other up;
>   And, gather'd into one,
> To our high calling's glorious hope
>   We hand in hand go on.[27]

The next failure that Wesley finds in Mysticism concerns the denial of the imputation of Christ's righteousness into the life of the believer. Or, one might say the conflict arises over the doctrine of the atonement, or the Mystics' lack of it.

The failure of the atonement is strikingly seen in the fact that the righteousness of Christ is not needed by their thought. True, the Mystics declare that we are not saved by our outer actions or good works, but Wesley charges them with saying we are saved by the works of our inner

---

25. Rattenbury, *Wesley's Legacy*, 122.

26. Lindstrom, *Wesley and Sanctification*, 130.

27. Wesley, *Wesley's Hymns*, no. 500, vv. 1–2.

righteousness. Man seeks justification or acceptance by God on account of his virtuous habits or tempers.

> Common writers suppose we are to be justified for the sake of our outward righteousness; these suppose we are to be justified for the sake of our inward righteousness; whereas, in truth, we are no more justified for the sake of one than of the other. . . . The sole cause of our acceptance with God . . . is the righteousness and the death of Christ, who fulfilled God's law, and died in our stead.[28]

Wesley will allow no foundation other than faith, trust, and confidence in Christ to be laid for the salvation of man. Works, inner or outer, have no power in the order of salvation to make a man acceptable to God. "Thus, at variance with exclusively contemplative, but in agreement with practical, mysticism, Wesley contends that both inward and outward holiness are necessary."[29]

Some of his opponents were unable to give a good account of the doctrine; they differed with Wesley largely because of their inability to understand him and their own doctrine. To them Wesley says:

> But still, though their opinions, as well as expressions, may be confused and inaccurate, their hearts may cleave to God through the Son of his love, and be truly interested in his righteousness.[30]

In a letter to Dr. William Robertson, Wesley calls the prime fallacy of the Mystics to be that of denying the doctrine of the atonement. They believe the Divinity incapable or unsusceptible of anger. This strikes at the roots of the doctrine of the atonement by making it unnecessary, and therefore, making unnecessary the doctrine of justification by faith, as taught by Wesley. This denial is sharply attacked by Wesley.[31] Wesley's hymnal is full of this denial.[32] All Christian believers are forgiven by God, justified, not because of any of their works, but by God's grace, God's imputation of Christ's righteousness to the believer. How is the righteousness of Christ imputed? Wesley answers:

28. Wesley, *Works*, 14:320.
29. Lindstrom, *Wesley and Sanctification*, 130.
30. Wesley, *Works*, 5:238.
31. Ibid., 12:214–15.
32. Wesley, *Wesley's Hymns*, no. 614, vv. 5–8, nos. 615–19.

All believers are forgiven and accepted, not for the sake of anything in them, or of anything that ever was, that is, or ever can be
done by them, but wholly and solely for the sake of what Christ
hath done and suffered for them. I say again, not for the sake of
anything in them, or done by them, of their own righteousness or
works: "Not for works of righteousness which we have done, but of
his own mercy he saved us."[33]

Lindstrom has excellently captured this argument between Wesley
and Law. Law has allowed the doctrine of atonement to suffer by allowing
man's self-mortification to be of help within the order of salvation. This
Wesley will not allow. The death on the cross, by Law's account, becomes
only a type of representational act performed in the name of mankind.
This is a type of salvation by faith *and* works and this concept Wesley
cannot accept.

Lindstrom rightly points out that Wesley makes the doctrine of the
atonement basic for his doctrine of justification, whereas Law makes
it more important for sanctification. According to Law, man and God
work for justification, and the prime emphasis is brought to bear upon
sanctification.

Wesley, then, came to regard Christ's work of atonement as the sole
ground of human justification. . . . Justification cannot therefore
be based on any righteousness in man himself: neither righteousness of outward acts nor righteousness of inward temper. Thus
sanctification becomes not a cause, but an effect, of justification.
Faith alone is regarded as the necessary condition for justification,
a faith which does not embrace any form of human sanctity, but
out of which inward and outward sanctity spring.[34]

Or, in the words of Wesley, we find the exact spirit that Lindstrom
has so well echoed:

And even the condition of it (acceptance with God) is not . . . our
holiness either of heart or life; but our faith alone; faith contradis-
tinguished from holiness, as well as from good works [parentheses
mine]. Other foundation therefore can no man lay, without being an adversary to Christ and his gospel, than faith alone; faith,

---

33. Wesley, *Works*, 5:239.

34. Lindstrom, *Wesley and Sanctification*, 59.

though necessarily producing both, yet not including either good works, or holiness.[35]

Wesley bases the entire Christian life upon faith—acceptance, trust, and reliance upon Christ. To this faith—but not as work—God gives forgiveness or justification as an act of His grace. To the continuing efforts of this faith—but not as a work—God gives the gift of sanctification. "There is no true faith, that is, justifying faith, which hath not the righteousness of Christ for its object."[36]

These are the major contentions between Wesley and the Mystics. However, there are numerous other differences, a few of which we will mention. The Mystics declared that every person passed through a period in which God was not known, a period that Wesley called the "wilderness state" or "heaviness."[37] In fact, the Mystics' taught that these periods were greatly to be desired, because a believer was able to increase rapidly in Christianity through them. Sugden comments:

> The Mystics believed that God deliberately withdrew Himself at times from their souls, so that they might learn to trust Him in the darkness and to fell their own helplessness without Him. Wesley's strong common sense could not accept this.[38]

Wesley will have no dealings with such interpretations as this. Relying upon the Scripture, to repeat a typical Wesleyan remark upon such an interpretation would be:

> The Scripture nowhere says, that the absence of God best perfected his work in the heart! Rather, his presence and a clear communion with the Father and the Son. A strong consciousness of this will do more in an hour, than his absence in an age.[39]

Wesley likewise cannot understand the typical Mystic's undervaluing of reason as an instrument of religious thought. The Mystics are placing Christianity in grave danger with their assertion that reason is not applicable to Christianity.

---

35. Wesley, *Works*, 14:320.

36. Ibid., 5:237.

37. Ibid., 6:77–91.

38. Wesley, *Standard Sermons*, 2:272–73.

39. Wesley, *Works*, 6:90.

> We find no authority for it (non use of reason) in holy writ [paren-
> theses mine]. So far from it, that we find there both our Lord and his
> Apostles continually reasoning with their opposes. . . . We therefore
> not only allow, but earnestly exhort all who seek after true religion,
> to use all the reason which God hath given them, in searching out
> the things of God. But your reasoning justly, not only on this, but
> on any subject whatsoever, pre-supposed true judgments already
> formed, whereon to ground your argumentation.[40]

Wesley attacks them in the same manner in his sermon, "The Case
of Reason Considered." This sermon directs the attention of his hearers
to the wonderful blessings reason brings to everyday life. Also, the same
is true about reason and the use of reason within religion. One cannot lay
the true foundation of religion without the proper use of reason. Neither
can one work for inner or outer holiness unless reason is a guide. He even
charges them with not promoting the cause of God because of their refusal to use reason in religious studies.

> Least of all, are you promoting the cause of God when you are
> endeavoring to exclude reason out of religion. Unless you willfully
> shut your eyes, you cannot but see of what service it is both in
> laying the foundation of true religion, under the guidance of the
> Spirit of God, and in raising the superstructure. You see it directs
> us in every point both of faith and practice: It guides us with re-
> gard to every branch both of inward and outward holiness.[41]

Finding its place within all of the former arguments, the final failure
which Wesley points out in the Mystic framework is well known by this
time. The Mystics do not rely upon the Scripture; the whole structure of
their thought is unscriptural. Because of this they have gotten themselves
into all of the other pitfalls. A proper study of the Scriptures, and the following of them, would have kept them out of the failures that have made
them a danger to True Christianity.

Wesley finds even the great Madam Guyon herself guilty of this
failure:

> The ground source of all her mistakes was this, the not being
> guided by the written word. She did not take the Scripture for the
> rule of her actions; at most it was but the secondary rule. Inward
> impressions were her primary rule. The written word was not a

40. Ibid., 8:12–13.
41. Ibid., 6:360.

lantern to her feet, a light in all her paths. No; she followed another light, the outward light of her confessors, and the inward light of her own spirit.[42]

Wesley always placed prime importance and authority upon the Scriptures themselves. Nothing else within Christianity was to take their place as the oracles of God. They stood supreme, and all else was to conform to the dictates of God contained therein.

> Wesley felt that the Scriptures should be read to find what they meant, though it is permissible always for an interpreter to tell us that his exegesis is what the Book suggests to him. One difficulty with mysticism always has been that, when the mystics have relied upon the Scriptures, they have interpreted the Scriptures in a fashion that the divine authors never could have recognized.[43]

The fact that the Mystics were not guided primarily by the Scriptures, and instead used them as a secondary guide, led to their use of words that were unscriptural. Wesley called himself a "Bible Bigot."[44] By this term he did not mean that no unscriptural word was adequate in religious matters. However, the Scriptures give to us the simplest and most direct language anywhere to be found, in discussing the elements of Christianity. Therefore, Wesley felt no compulsion to think up other words to describe the experiences and beliefs that the Scripture discusses so well. Wesley seemed to think, why not make use of the plain and original words?

Wesley more than once gave his opinion that Jacob Behmen was so utterly difficult to read that he was hardly worth the time spent in so doing. Even when Law gave some shape to the Behmen writings, giving them a more palatable form, Wesley did not like spending the time necessary to work through the abridged form. Wesley attacked the whole phraseology of Behmen as not being useful.

> It is both unscriptural, and affectedly mysterious. I say, affectedly; for this does not necessarily result from the nature of the things spoken of. St. John speaks as high and as deep things as Jacob Behmen. Why then does not Jacob speak as plain as him?[45]

42. Ibid., 14:277.
43. McConnell, *John Wesley*, 151.
44. Wesley, *Letters*, 5:313.
45. Wesley, *Works*, 3:160.

In his "Thoughts Upon Jacob Behmen," Wesley summarizes his disagreements with this Mystic.[46] The whole foundation of Behmen's thought is wrong, because it is based upon and complicated with a philosophical theory. Wesley objects to explaining Christianity by the method of any philosophy. But even so, Behmen does not do anything with the foundation he has made—he presents nothing that is not already known before. Behmen uses language that confuses rather than helps the reader. The whole system becomes useless, mischievous; striking at the root of humility and external religion as well as all revealed religion; by making the Bible less than it ought to be.[47]

In the words of John Fletcher Hurst:

> He objected to many of the mystic writers, he tells us, because they appear to have no conception of Church communion, depreciate the means of grace, are wise above what is written, and, indulging in unscriptural speculations, are apt to despise all who differ from them as carnal, unenlightened men. Their whole phraseology was both unscriptural and affectedly mysterious. . . . While Wesley appreciated some great spiritual truths emphasized by the mystics, he rejected the speculative and sentimental errors which afterward marred the work of the Moravians. If Methodism had become mysticism, it would have lacked the force for the moral revolution which England needed.[48]

MYSTICISM AND SALVATION

There is no doubt about Wesley as to his view of the possibility of salvation for the Mystics. Again we see that Wesley contends for the reality of the experience, rather than the outer form of expressing that experience. A man may be entirely wrong in his structuring the saving experience, and yet have a vital, intimate, personal, moment-by-moment fellowship with Christ.

The Mystics' resistance to Scripture appalls Wesley; their straying from the True Christianity that he preaches and their deviations from the community of Christ shock him. But, he is not willing to dispose of these differences by declaring that the holder of these concepts is therefore un-

---

46. Ibid., 9:509–14.

47. Ibid.

48. Hurst, *History of Methodism*, 314–15.

fit for salvation. A classic statement is found in the sermon "The Lord our Righteousness."

> But will any one dare to affirm that all Mystics, (such as Mr. Law in particular), all Quakers, all Presbyterians or Independents, and all members of the church of England who are not clear in their opinions or expressions, are void of all Christian experience?—that consequently, they are all in a state of damnation, "without hope, without God in the world?" However confused their ideas may be, however improper their language, may there not be many of them whose heart is right toward God, and who effectually know "the Lord our righteousness?"[49]

Wesley followed the same train of thought in many of his controversies. It is a remarkable piece of writing that finds its way into his *Journal* for November 30, 1767. In this consideration, Wesley makes it clear once again that the ability to structure the doctrine rightly, and the experience that has brought the doctrine into existence are not the same. Salvation is not wrought by the ability of one to structure the doctrine, rather is the gift of God's grace. He writes:

> That a man may be saved, who has not clear conceptions of it (Imputed Righteousness) [parentheses mine]. Therefore, clear conceptions of it are not necessary to salvation: Yes, it is not necessary to salvation to use the phrase at all:
> That a pious Churchman who has not clear conceptions even of Justification by Faith may be saved. Therefore, clear conceptions even of this are not necessary to salvation:
> That a Mystic, who denies Justification by Faith, (Mr. Law, for instance,) may be saved.[50]

Here we find a natural progression of thought. A man is saved not by his ability to structure doctrine, but by the saving relationship that he has with God. Therefore it is obvious that one need not be clear in his doctrine—this is salvation by thought formulations. He need not even seek to affirm the doctrine of justification by faith; he may be utterly opposed to it. But, if he has the reality for which the doctrine is contending, salvation is his, regardless of theological error.

49. Wesley, *Works*, 5:243.
50. Ibid., 3:308.

Repeatedly Wesley affirms this contention. At least twice in his "Remarks on Mr. Hill's Review" this affirmation is made.[51] "Now, although Mr. Law denied justification by faith, he might trust in the merits of Christ. It is this, and this only, that I affirm . . ."[52] Again, in "Remarks on Mr. Hill's Farrago Double—Distilled,"[53] in the same controversy, Wesley says, "Now, although Mr. Law denied justification by faith, he might trust in the merits of Christ. It is this, and this only, that I affirm . . ."[54]

The Mystic is a Christian, admittedly a rather odd one with a wide variety of peculiarities, but nonetheless, a Christian. As such, he may trust in Christ for his salvation and be rewarded with God's gift of the same.

MYSTICISM AND "TRUE CHRISTIANITY"

Wesley, the protagonist of True Christianity is ever wary of the Mystics and their experiences. Though nearly shipwrecking his faith upon their mistakes early in life, once he got his bearings, he never came close to trouble again.

In Wesleyan theology, the means of grace receive great prominence.[55] The brothers always contend for the use of the means of grace. Through their lives they communed regularly and often. Charles wrote 166 hymns on the Lord's Supper, which have been collected by Rattenbury.[56]

In his sermon on "The Means of Grace," Wesley gives pointed instruction as to how the Christian should use these means. He points out that Christ institutes the means and man should therefore use them for the purpose God gave them to be used. For example:

> Is not the eating of that bread, and the drinking of that cup, the outward, visible means whereby God conveys into our souls all that spiritual grace, that righteousness, and peace, and joy in the Holy Ghost, which were purchased by the body of Christ once broken, and the blood of Christ once shed for us? Let all, therefore,

51. Ibid., 10:374–414.
52. Ibid., 10:391, 403.
53. Ibid., 10:415–46.
54. Ibid., 10:433.
55. Wesley, *Wesley's Hymns*, nos. 546–52.
56. Rattenbury, *Eucharistic Hymns*, 195–249.

who truly desire the grace of God, eat of that bread, and drink of that cup.[57]

The importance of the means of grace is found in many of the communion hymns of the Wesley's. One such hymn is:

> O God of truth and love,
> Let us Thy mercy prove;
> Bless Thine ordinance Divine,
> Let it now effectual be,
> Answer all its great design,
> All the gracious ends in me.
>
> O might the sacred word
> Set forth our dying Lord,
> Point us to Thy suffering past,
> Present grace and strength impart,
> Give our ravish'd souls a taste,
> Pledge of glory in our heart.
>
> Come in Thy Spirit down,
> Thine institution grown;
> Lamb of God, as slain appear,
> Life of all believers Thou,
> Let us now perceive Thee near,
> Come, Thou Hope of glory, now.[58]

The True Christian seeks the ends of Christianity using all the means God has given to him to use. He does not live apart from the institutional representation of Christianity as found in the church. For him, the church is a vital part of his life. Wesley believes that in some ways the grace of God works only through the fellowship of the church. Only in this fellowship is found the fullness of the relationship of God with man, and man with his brother.

Christianity is unashamedly an automatically institutional or communal centered religion. Christianity cannot long live apart from the community of Christ. The Quietism or apartness of the Mystics is denounced by Wesley because there are demands upon the Christian made by Christ that have to be carried on within community, they are impossible to fulfill

57. Wesley, *Standard Sermons*, 1:253.

58. Rattenbury, *Eucharistic Hymns*, 211.

outside community.[59] McConnell captures the double-headed attack of Wesley upon the Mystic mistakes:

> One count was the disregard of means, the expectation of ends without the use of the instruments appropriate to secure the ends. Another was the tendency to a false waiting upon God, a quietism which cost nothing in exertion.[60]

So far is separation from True Christianity that Wesley can say the great reason why Christians are in the world is that God's grace may be communicated through them to others. The whole life of the True Christian is to help influence the nonbelievers as much as possible.

> This is the great reason why the providence of God has so mingled you together with other men, that whatever grace you have received of God may through you be communicated to others; that every holy temper and word and work of yours may have an influence on them also. By this means a check will, in some measure, be given to the corruption which is in the world; and a small part, at least, saved from the general infection, and rendered holy and pure before God.[61]

Even after all this is done and said, Wesley has a great fear of the misleading of Mysticism. So powerful an influence is it that he says in XIX of his *Standard Sermons*:

> After all that Scripture and reason have said, so exceeding plausible are the pretences for solitary religion, for a Christian's going out of the world, or at least hiding himself in it, that we need all the wisdom of God to see through the snare, and all the power of God to escape it, so many and strong are the objections which have been brought against being social, open, active Christians.[62]

Being a "Bible Bigot" cost Wesley much exertion. Had he not believed the Bible in the way in which he did, he could have lived his life apart from others and enjoyed the sweet communion with God in quietness. However, his study of the Scripture led him to see that some of the basic commands of Christ, such as loving one's neighbor as oneself, can only be fulfilled if one has a neighbor near enough to love. Therefore, Wesley felt

59. Wesley, *Standard Sermons*, 1:382
60. McConnell, *John Wesley*, 150.
61. Wesley, *Standard Sermons*, 1:385.
62. Ibid., 1:390.

a compulsion to activity and service within the community of Christ. He was called into action and never ceased until, on his deathbed, he uttered the words, "The best of all is God is with us."

Never one to quibble over words, Wesley probably wished he hadn't had many of his fights. His *Journal* is full of notations that he would not fight with one, or that he regretted having to contend with another. Fighting over the reality of the Christian experience, and only secondly for the wording of the doctrine, he could offer the hand of Christian fellowship to those who were extremely different in doctrinal interpretation from himself.

It is a part of his greatness that he is able to penetrate to the very core of Christianity, rather than be caught up in the outer periphery and lose himself in a battle over words with his opponents. The plain, simple Christianity caught him and he never let it go.

The battle over the authority within Christianity was one that Wesley might well have thought he would not have to fight. However, the times were not right. He lived in days in which the Bible was not automatically accepted as the authority for Christianity. From his position, it was probably painful to see so many of his countrymen seeking to be Christian, but removing themselves so far away from the God-given foundation of Christianity in the Scripture.[63]

The proper foundation for Christianity is Christ, as found in Scripture and interpreted by the Church over the centuries. The basic study of the Christian is the Scripture, the means of interpretation or the guide.[64] The final authority is Christ mediated though the Scriptures and made intelligible through the Holy Spirit and the believer's reason.

The reality of the experience of the Mystic and Wesley is not extremely different. But, the means used by each, and the doctrinal affirmations of the experience, are poles apart. Only the keen insight of Wesley and an abundant outpouring of God's grace permit him to place first things first.

An excellent example of Wesley's debate with other Christians on an *opinion* is that concerning the imputation of Christ's righteousness

63. Wesley, *Wesley's Hymns*, nos. 88, 255.
64. Ibid., no. 746.

to the believer, by God. This Wesley firmly believed, yet considered it to be an opinion.[65]

His sermon "The Lord Our Righteousness" presents his view of the matter. It is a key doctrine of the Church, for the Church stands or falls upon this doctrine.[66] All Christian faith has, as a consequence, the righteousness of Christ imputed to the believer.[67]

Yet, even with this strong emphasis upon the righteousness of Christ, he still says that those who give different opinions as to the doctrine are not consigned to hell because of it. The difference lies more in *opinion*, but especially in *expression of the opinion*, than it does in the *reality* of the believers' experience with God.

> But if the difference be more in *opinion*, than real *experience*, and more in expression than in opinion, how can it be, that even the children of God should so vehemently contend with each other on the point? Several reasons may be assigned for this: The chief is, their not understanding one another; joined with too keen an attachment to their opinions, and particular modes of expression.[68]

In fighting for an intimate, personal union with God, Wesley fought side by side with the Mystic. The difference is that Wesley thinks the union was brought into being by use of the means of grace and was strengthened by continued use of them. Agreeing that union with God was primary and the root of religion, he further states that "if this root be really in the heart, it cannot but put forth branches."[69] These branches are the outward obedience of the Christian, which has the same nature as the root of religion. "Consequently, they are not only means or signs, but substantial parts, of religion."[70] These branches are one part of True Christianity and contemplation is another. The True Christian does not follow one to the exclusion of the other.[71] The Mystics, on the other hand, thought the union of God with man was so important, it overrode all other considerations and because of this emphasis were led astray into a

---

65. Wesley, *Works*, 5:238.

66. Ibid., 5:235.

67. Ibid., 5:236.

68. Ibid.

69. Wesley, *Standard Sermons*, 1:390.

70. Ibid.

71. Ibid., 1:393.

multitude of problems. Wesley could well end his controversy with the words of his brother:

> From our own inventions vain
>> Of fancied happiness,
> Draw us to thyself again,
>> And bid our wanderings cease;
> Jesus speak our souls restored,
>> By Love's divine simplicity;
> Re-united to our Lord,
>> And wholly lost in thee![72]

---

72. Wesley, *Wesley's Hymns*, no. 98, v. 2.

8

Conclusion

T HERE WE HAVE DONE it; we are done with our look at Wesley's thought about other religions and the aberrations of Christianity from within. Attacked from without and scuttled from within, Wesley still fought for True Christianity. This theme filled his whole life and thought.[1]

WESLEY'S VIEW OF CHRISTIANITY

Christianity seeks an intimate, personal, dynamic relationship between God and man, as made possible by Christ.[2] This experience is bounded by the authority of Scripture and helped to intelligible interpretation by man's reason.[3] Religious experience with God—the Christian God, as interpreted by Scripture and reason—is the basic fundamental aspect of True Christianity.

> This is only the outside of that religion which he insatiably hungers after. The knowledge of God in Christ Jesus; the life which is hid with Christ in God; the being "joined unto the Lord in one spirit"; the having "fellowship with the Father and the Son"; the "walking in the light as God is in the light"; the being "purified even as He is pure,"—this is the religion, the righteousness he thirsts after; nor can he rest, till he thus rests in God.[4]

This intimate relationship is made possible not as the wages for man's work, but as the free gift of God's grace. Man is spiritually bankrupt before God in the order of salvation and must receive, as a gift, this saving relationship whereby Christ's righteousness is given to us and our sin

1. Wesley, *Works*, 6:428, 10:72–75.
2. Wesley, *Wesley's Hymns*, no. 97.
3. Wesley, *Works*, 6:354–55.
4. Wesley, *Standard Sermons*, 1:344.

forgiven.[5] It is begun by prevenient grace, the first tugs of God on our hearts to read of Him, to listen to Him, to recognize Him. No matter what it is called, the reality of this experience is fundamental to the Christian life. This is walking in eternity.[6]

From the center of love, holy tempers, words of mercy, works of purity, and fellowship in the Church radiate in importance.[7]

The fruit of this relationship is "righteousness, peace, and joy in the Holy Spirit." The fruit of this relationship is also loving God with heart, soul, mind, and strength, and loving one's neighbor as oneself.[8] The fruit of this love is shown and interpreted by Christ, both in his life and in his teachings. The love of God is to be shed to all our acquaintances, by the work of the Spirit of God.

The fruit is founded upon the repeated use of the instituted means of grace, which God has given to the community of Christ. These instituted means are not to be slighted, because they are God given. One cannot fulfill Christianity without using them, for they are the foundations of the Christian life.

The pull of Christianity is always towards further growth in the grace of God.[9] One seeks not only forgiveness for sin and acceptance by God, justification; but we seek further growth in grace until we love God and man fully, sanctification. Lindstrom has captured and expressed this excellently, but Cannon has missed it. A short statement is found in Wesley's *Standard Sermons* LXXXV.

> Afterwards (after *preventing* and *convincing* graces and *repentance)*, we experience the proper Christian salvation; whereby, "through grace," we "are saved by faith;" consisting of those two grand branches, justification and sanctification [parentheses mine]. By justification we are saved from the guilt of sin, and restored to the favour of God; by sanctification we are saved from the power and root of sin, and restored to the image of God. All experience, as well as Scripture, show this salvation to be both instantaneous and gradual. It begins the moment we are justified, in the holy, humble, gentle, patient love of God and man. It gradually increases from

5. Wesley, *Works*, 6:508–9.

6. Ibid., 6:196.

7. Ibid., 7:60, 64–65.

8. Ibid., 6:162.

9. Wesley, *Wesley's Hymns*, nos. 340–417; *Standard Sermons*, 2:97.

that moment, as "a grain of mustard-seed, which, at first, is the least of all seeds," but afterwards puts forth large branches and becomes a great tree; till, in another instant, the heart is cleansed from all sin, and filled with pure love to God and man. But even that love increases more and more, till we "grow up in all things into Him that is our Head;" till we attain "the measure of the stature of the fullness of Christ."[10]

This, as a skeletal framework, will supply us with a jumping-point from Wesley's view of Christianity to the other religions and to the corruptions of Christianity. We will now examine the response of Wesley to those outside Christianity and then to those within the borders of Christianity.

THOSE OUTSIDE CHRISTIANITY—OTHER RELIGIONS

To those of other world religions, Wesley first would urge that we apply the prevenient grace of God. Even to the Heathen, the man by definition apart from God, he would urge the application of this doctrine. No man lives entirely apart from the grace of God. It is impossible to escape from the love of God, even in the Heathen's existence.[11]

The magnetic pull of Wesleyan theology towards the doctrine of Entire Sanctification is found even in its first stages of prevenient grace.[12] These are the first urgings of God that a man turn to Him and be saved, the first response of man to please God. The man of another religion is not without this witness in the world.

We have seen that Wesley prefers the term *preventing grace* to the more common term *natural conscience*. The reason is obvious in Wesleyan theology, for Wesley believes that this is not something *naturally* inherent within man, but the gift of God to every man. As a gift of God's grace, it cannot be understood to be purely a natural thing, something inalienably present within the nature of man, apart from the workings of God.

Wesley points out that God is not a respecter of persons. He does not want God to be understood as one who elects some people to be saved and some damned, for this makes of God something far less than he can find by the study of Scripture. The fight with the Calvinists ought to have

10. Wesley, *Works*, 6:509.

11. Ibid., 6:506.

12. Ibid., 6:509–10.

clearly taught us this principle, but we have not always followed the conclusions it brings. God wants the Heathen, the Jews and the Mohammedan
to be saved.[13] This is the way in which Wesley shows that all are saved
through Christ. They may not know it, but His is the Name by which the
salvation of mankind has been purchased. There is no other name under
heaven by which salvation is to be found for men. Know it or not, this is
the basis of every man's salvation.

> But in every nation he that feareth him, and worketh righteous-
> ness—He that first reverence God, as great, wise, good; the Cause,
> End, and Governor of all things; and, secondly, from this awful
> regard to Him, not only avoids all known evil, but endeavors, ac-
> cording to the best light he has, to do all things well. Is accepted
> of him—through Christ, though he knows Him not. The asser-
> tion is express, and admits of no exception. He is in the favour of
> God, whether enjoying His written word and ordinances or not.
> Nevertheless, the addition of these is an unspeakable blessing to
> those who were before, in some measure, accepted; otherwise, God
> would never have sent an angel from heaven to direct Cornelius
> to St. Peter.[14]

Here we have, in distilled form, the basic Wesleyan affirmation of the
relationship between Christianity and the other religions.

The prevenient grace of God melts into further graces, but always
God is no respecter of persons. Always God seeks the salvation of His
whole creation.

> I perceive of a truth—More clearly than ever, from such a concur-
> rence of circumstances. That God is not a respecter of persons—Is
> not partial in His love. The words mean, in a particular sense, that
> He does not confine His love to one nation; in general, that He is
> loving to every man, and willeth all men should be saved.[15]

Clearly, Wesley thinks that the whole creation of God's is being
worked over by God Himself, in His efforts to save all men.

Always, Wesley thinks man is responsible before God. Man has a
part in his own salvation. Though he is utterly incapable of saving himself,
without his response to the grace of God, salvation cannot be his. In ev-

---

13. Wesley, *Wesley's Hymns*, no. 164, v. 6.
14. Wesley, *Notes*, 434–35.
15. Ibid., 434.

ery act by which man accepts the grace of God rather than rejecting this grace, man is said to be a cooperator with God. This cooperation is not a work of merit, rather, it is the acceptance of the loving forgiveness freely offered by God to man. Man cannot save himself, but he can choose not to be separated from God and in so doing, prevent himself from being condemned.

Man is responsible before God. He does not have the ability within himself to respond to God and to thereby save himself. Man is responsible because the grace of God is offered to him and he has the power to accept or refuse it. Man has a significant choice to make—for or against receiving the love of God.

Though a man receive but an extremely weak ray of light from God, it nonetheless is the Light of God and must be accepted as such. Being true to this light is enough to save a man. Man must be true to the light that has been given him, and though it be but the weakest light of prevenient grace, it is enough.[16] "Toward those who have never tasted of the good Lord, God is indeed pitiful and of tender mercy."[17]

Thus, in the case of the Heathen, salvation is the gift of God to him, though the Heathen has not offered himself knowingly to Jesus as the Christ. He has accepted and responded to the light of the prevenient grace of God.[18] Thus, is the case of Muslims. They have not accepted the God known in Christ as such. But, the light that the Muslim has through his religion is faintly the Light of God through Christ. It is strangely weird and twisted from the Christian perspective, but nonetheless, it is the Light of God, and for one to accept this light and act upon it, is to receive salvation.

Thus again, we find the same true in the case of the Jew. If the Jewish people follow the dispensation that God has given them, they are in the relationship with Him termed salvation. This dispensation has been given by God and is to be accepted by them. If the Jews accept it and follow it as the Light of God, it is for them, salvation.[19]

The main argument of Wesley against the Jew at this point is that he has not lived up to the light that he has. Arguing from the Old Testament, Wesley points out their failures in following the living Light of God. To be sure, the more complete and final fullness of light is found in Christianity,

16. Williams, *John Wesley's Theology Today*, 45.

17. Wesley, *Standard Sermons*, 1:386.

18. Wesley, *Works*, 6:508–9.

19. Wesley, *Wesley's Hymns*, no. 452, v. 4.

but enough for salvation is found in the other religions. This is not to say that Wesley thought all religions equal or all of them to be considered along with Christianity as one of many ways to the same goal.

Though he dares not to say they cannot be saved, he has definite opinions concerning the uniqueness of Christianity and its strength in the face of the other religions' weaknesses. As to salvation, the final answer that Wesley often gives is that we must wait for the decision of God.[20] This, in the final analysis, is but to state the obvious, for we find ourselves in judgment before God and not our fellow man.

He stands in a good position by saying that man dare not exclude God from working in places other than those which men have been able to see and understand. God has given more than one dispensation, according to Wesley anyway, and to make God's grace stop at the borders of Christianity is greatly limiting God! Not only that, but we have seen that Wesley always considers the whole of mankind the creation of God and within His interest for salvation.

God is seeking to bring the totality of man to Himself. His prevenient grace is active and present in all. The death of God's Son upon the cross was not just for a few, but also for the whole world. These things being true, it is almost impossible for one to maintain that God stops short at the borders of the Christian religion. The problem now becomes that of considering how God will work beyond the borders of Christianity.

Wesley's emphasis upon the order of salvation makes him seek to bring in those of other religions as well as those without religion, if there can be such. From the basis of original sin, the infecting separation of man from God, which has made its way from Adam to his modern descendents, God is working to relieve and forgive us. Prevenient grace wipes this slate clean; for Wesley believes that none will die or forever be separate from God singly on account of original sin. Prevenient grace is present and active in all men, seeking to start them up the magnetically pulling order of salvation until they reach the highest within the order of salvation is reached, Christian perfection.

Wesley's view of atonement in the order of salvation makes him want to bring the other peoples of the world into a saving relationship with God. The atonement that God worked through Christ is for the whole world,

---

20. Wesley, *Works*, 8:353.

not just for a few. Christ died that the whole world, which was separated from God, might now be brought to Him and be reconciled to Him.[21]

Justification and sanctification are open, by the grace of God, to those who have put on the garments of repentance and have sought the forgiveness of God. The growth of grace in sanctification is the goal of every Christian. The prominence in Wesley, upon the order of salvation, makes it necessary for him to think in terms of a universal religion. Christianity is not just for the English and for the American. Christ is for the whole world, and wherever a man is saved it is through Christ. The man may not know it, but Christ is the basis, everywhere, for salvation. Living up to the light he has in his religion is enough for salvation, because the light in that religion is Christ. Wesley is Christocentric, basing Christianity and salvation squarely upon the works of atonement, which God has made available to the total of mankind through Christ.

Wesley is certain that Christianity is for all mankind. Adam signified the fall of the whole human race from that intimate, dynamic, living, and vital relationship with God. Adam speaks of our spiritual depravity, our corruption, our rebellion, our denial. Adam is the totality of mankind as estranged from a living and saving relationship with God.

Even as Adam is all men, so Christ is for all men. Even as in Adam all are dead, so in Christ, all may live. The first section of *Wesley's Hymns*, 1780, and the *Notes* adequately point this out.

God has called every sinner to the gospel feast to be found in Christ:

> Sent by my Lord, on you I call;
> The invitation is to ALL;
> Come, all the world; come, sinner, *thou*;
> All things in Christ are ready now.
>
> Come, all ye souls by sin opprest,
> Ye restless wanderers after rest,
> Ye poor, and maim'd and halt, and blind,
> In Christ a hearty welcome find.
>
> Ye vagrant souls, on you I call;
> (O that my voice could reach you all!)
> Ye all may now be justified;
> Ye all may live, for Christ hath died.

21. Wesley, *Wesley's Hymns*, no. 190, v. 5.

My message as from God receive;
Ye all may come to Christ, and live;
O let his love your hearts constrain,
Nor suffer him to die in vain!

This is the time; no more delay;
This is the acceptable day;
Come in, this moment, at his call,
And live for him who died for all.[22]

The promises are for all,[23] the Savior for all,[24] and the grace of God for all.[25] God would receive the whole world, but man will not have it so.[26]

To Wesley, there is only one religion, only one proper way to God. This way God has Himself given to man by His Son. All other so-called "religions," are only broken lights, irrationally constructed. Were one faced with True Christianity, Wesley is almost naively certain that they will accept the greater light even though he has seen abundant evidence to the contrary.

Since there is one humanity, which is the creation of one God, and one Savior of this humanity, there is the one religion, Christianity, which God has given to His children. To those outside Christianity the message is Christ.[27] The light of salvation is Christ. All is Christ. He seeks to present the mercy of God for mankind, as revealed through the work of Jesus. This is the method used in the hymns and the message he gives as being the basis of his pulpit work. There are "orders" or "circles" of divine providence. The first "order" concerns the totality of mankind.[28]

THOSE INSIDE CHRISTIANITY—INNER CORRUPTIONS

To those within Christianity, Wesley is always an advocate of True Religion or True Christianity. In this position he never fails to let his opponents know about the dangerous condition of the inner corruptions of Christianity.

22. Ibid., no. 2, vv. 1–3, 5–6, 9.

23. Ibid., no. 4, v. 8.

24. Ibid., no. 10, v. 3.

25. Ibid., no. 4, v. 2.

26. Ibid., no. 6.

27. Wesley, *Works*, 7:264, 271–72.

28. Ibid., 6:319, 428.

By force of Scripture and reason he seeks all means open to him to bring them into True Christianity. He enforces his own position to show the places in which his brothers have strayed in their thoughts and actions. Using the method of squarely basing all of his thought upon the Scriptures, he is able to pinpoint the corruptions of Christianity, show precisely where they have strayed, and discuss how to cure their sickness. The place of the Scriptures in Wesleyan theology is well shown by a hymn.

> Father of mercies, in thy word
>> What endless glory shines!
> For ever be thy name adored
>> For these celestial lines.
>
> Here may the wretched sons of want
>> Exhaustless riches find;
> Riches, above what earth can grant,
>> And lasting as the mind.
>
> Here the fair Tree of Knowledge grows,
>> And yields a free repast;
> Sublimer sweets than nature knows,
>> Invite the longing taste.
>
> Here the Redeemer's welcome voice
>> Spreads heavenly peace around;
> And life and everlasting joys
>> Attend the blissful sound.
>
> Divine Instructor, gracious Lord,
>> Be thou for ever near;
> Teach me to love thy sacred word,
>> And view my Saviour there.[29]

By temperament he would rather have remained out of many of the controversies into which he was pulled. His preference is to just consign them to God and let things be handled in that manner. However, such cannot be the case many times, in actual human life. He thinks it imperative that he answer them for fear that others within Methodism will think the Methodist position is invalid or cannot be held against the charges of others.

29. Wesley, *Wesley's Hymns,* no. 746.

In his controversies, he writes private letters to his antagonists with more detailed information than he put in the published letters. In these letters he corrects their mistakes, misquotes, and other errata. Some of these letters might have been extremely embarrassing to some of his foes, but many of them came back again and again for a dose of the same at the hands of a master practical theologian.

When thoroughly aroused that Christianity hangs in the balance, he will attack, with honor and within bounds, but the strength of his argument can hardly be weakened.

He will use the Scriptures to the best advantage possible, and reason extremely ably. His attack will change with the importance of the controversy to Christianity. If it is not too important, he will not argue the point and will give many of the points away that he normally contends.

Wesley always refuses to condemn his opponents, to declare that they have no possibility for salvation because of their differences with him and True Christianity. Some of his opponents write in a manner that leads one to doubt whether this gesture is appreciated by and always returned by them.

Believing in the personal, intimate union of God with man, along the lines of the Scripture, he will rather leave the salvation of the person to God. Often, he refuses to damn or condemn them, or allow his followers to say that a certain position is enough for one to conclude the impossibility of salvation for the holder of it.

It is always his contention that the person is held in account to God. He is to be tried by the light he has and his stewardship of that light. Wesley is aware that the Light of God is a difficult thing for the mind of man to grasp and is very willing to change his opinions—provided he can be shown sufficient cause by Scripture and reason.

Again and again we have seen that he will declare an opponent to have opinions extremely wide of the mark. Yet he will not declare the impossibility of their salvation. The True Christian experience could be present within the individual, even if their doctrinal affirmation is weak, contradictory, and wide of the mark.

Part of this leniency of Wesley's must be seen against the backdrop of his counting the experience with God as primary and the formulation of this experience secondary. He spoke highly of doctrinal truths, but doctrinal truths are not equivalent to, nor to be confused with, salvation. Man is not saved by his doctrinal affirmations or conceptions; the only salvation comes to man as the gift of God's grace through Christ. This is a relationship and a fellowship with God out of which grows the fruit of the Spirit. If the fruit of the Spirit is found within the individual, Wesley is not going to argue that the doctrinal affirmations are wrong enough to keep the individual out of heaven.

This just points up the fact that Wesley believed in salvation by faith, not salvation by doctrine. True doctrine receives a high commendation by Wesley—he fought for it all his life. Even so the Christian is not saved by his doctrine, but by his trust, confidence, and obedience to the Light of God, as it is given and received through Christ.

The first method employed against those within Christianity is the use of Scripture. By their being a Christian, Wesley assumes that the Scriptures will have a special place. He likewise assumes their living in a closer relationship to God than the Heathen or those of other religions.[30] Yet, he believes the True Christian to be closest in God's providence.[31] To Wesley, the Scriptures carry the highest authority. If his antagonists will only follow the Scriptures, as does Wesley, he thinks they will not have so many controversies.

FINAL CONCLUSIONS

In a final, quick summary of the results of this book, we must discuss three distinctive contributions of Wesley. His distinction between the *fact* and the *manner* of a doctrine, whereby one may believe a doctrine though he does not know perfectly all ramifications of it, is extremely valuable. As Wesley himself says, who knows fully and is able to adequately explain the doctrine of the Trinity? Yet, we all are aware of the *fact*.

Wesley's distinction between *doctrines* and *opinions* is a contribution which could well come in for additional theological study today. By making this distinction, we could avoid many possible pitfalls in ecumenical studies, and even in the work of the local churches throughout the world.

The contribution of the prevenient grace of God is worthy of study today, as well. This doctrine makes better sense than some of the more harsh interpretations of Calvinism on the one hand or the belief that all will be saved on the other. It also gives us basis for more work upon the doctrines of man and the grace of God.

30. Wesley, *Works*, 6:319.
31. Ibid., 6:319–20, 428–29.

Further conclusions find a place at this time. Wesley's emphasis upon a man being judged only by the light he has received from God and his obedience to it is important for us to recognize. Our day is one in which we deal with other religions, and we need some background for our interpretation of them. This may not be an adequate, or fully worked out presentation, but it bears future study.

Along the same lines is his emphasis that the light they have is the Light of God as revealed through Christ, whether the person recognizes it or not. The firm Christocentric basis of his whole theology is worthy of our consideration and commendation.

The distinction between one's religion and the possibility of salvation has been pointed out in our study. One may have a religion that is based upon an exceedingly weak reflection of the Light of God, and yet, by obedience to that light, receive salvation. Religion is poor, but the obedience is worthy, making salvation the gift of God to the man of faith.[32]

There are many religions, so-called, but in deepest reality all of them have but faint and dim reflection of God's Light in Christ. They do not have an independent existence, all to themselves, wholly apart from Christ. They are one of the various dispensations from God; all based upon Christ, the Son of God.

As there is one mankind, the creation of one God; so there is one religion for this mankind, Christianity. Christianity is the religion built around the unique Son of God, the gift of God's grace to the whole world, the totality of mankind. Man is made for one happiness—communion with Him.[33]

> What could your redeemer do,
> More than he hath done for you?
> To procure your peace with God
> Could he more than shed his blood?
> After all his waste of love,
> All his drawings from above,
> Why will you your Lord deny?
> Why will you resolve to die?

32. Ibid., 7:354.
33. Ibid., 6:431.

Turn, he cries, ye sinners turn"
By his life your God hath sworn,
He would have you turn and live,
He would all the world receive.
If your death were his delight,
Would he you to life invite?
Would he ask, obtest, and cry,
Why will you resolve to die?[34]

34. Wesley, *Wesley's Hymns*, no. 8, vv. 1–2.

Study Guide

SCRIPTURE

All scripture is inspired by God and is useful for teaching, for reproof, for correction, and for training in righteousness, so that everyone who belongs to God may be proficient, equipped for every good work.

2 TIMOTHY 3:16–18

PRAYER

Our Heavenly Father, who has put a curiosity and drive to learn within us, be with us as we start our study together. We have searched through your creation trying to learn all we can and this search will never be satisfied until it, too, finds its rest in you. Bless us as we think together, discuss together, and share our ideas and life experiences with each other through our studies. We ask these things in the name of our Christ. Amen.

INTRODUCTION

1. What does the author say is the purpose of the book?

2. What are the "isms" that we will be studying?

3. What resource materials are basic to this study?

Read at least fifty pages in one of them to get a sample or taste of John Wesley's writings.

4. How does Wesley define the *fact* and *manner* of doctrines? Can you give an example that would illustrate this difference? How does this distinction help you understand doctrines better?

5. What does Wesley mean by *doctrines* and *opinions*? Can you give an example?

6. Wesley offers two possible definitions of salvation. How do they differ? Does one sound better to you than the other? Why?

7. What role do hymns play in the theology of John Wesley's Methodists?

NOTES

SCRIPTURE

Yet you have made them a little lower than God,
  and crowned them with glory and honor.
You have given them dominion over the works of your hands;
  you have put all things under their feet,
All sheep and oxen,
  and also the beasts of the field,
The birds of the air, and the fish of the sea,
  whatever passes along the paths of the seas.

O Lord, our Sovereign,
  how majestic is your name in all the earth!

PSALM 8:5–9

PRAYER

O God, who has created us, and put within us a desire to know you; we thank you. O God, who has known us from our conception and followed us until today and who will follow us into the future, we thank you. O God, whose grace has sought to enlighten us, to turn us to you, to stir in us an answer to your love, we thank you. Bless us as we study together that we might enjoy our fellowship with you and those who study together. In Christ's name we pray Amen.

CHAPTER 1. NATURAL MAN AND PREVENIENT GRACE

1. Wesley discusses the image of God. How has the image of God changed as a result of the fall of man?

2. What are the chances that Natural Man can be saved?

3. What does Wesley think about the existence of Natural Man?

4. How does Wesley handle the Fall that is different from most scholars today?

5. How does Wesley define sin?

6. Even though man has fallen, in what areas does Wesley think he is still able to work effectively? In what areas is he unable to do anything effectively?

7. What does Wesley mean by *prevenient grace*?

8. How does Wesley relate man's conscience with prevenient grace?

9. How does the doctrine of prevenient grace keep Wesley from extreme Calvinism?

10. How does man's response to God's grace prevent it (the response) from becoming a work of salvation?

11. In what way is man responsible for being "saved"?

NOTES

SCRIPTURE

*But God, who is rich in mercy, out of the great love with which he loved us,
even when we were dead through our trespasses, made us alive together
with Christ—by grace you have been saved—and raised us up with him
and seated us with him in the heavenly places in Christ Jesus, so that in the
ages to come he might show the immeasurable riches of his grace in kind-
ness toward us in Christ Jesus. For by grace you have been saved through
faith, and this is not your own doing; it is the gift of God—not the result
of works, so that no one may boast.*

EPHESIANS 2:4–8

PRAYER

Almighty God, from whom we have received grace upon grace, we give
you thanks for the love which has called us from a life of sin to a life
of abundant grace. Bless us as we consider how your love even today
is pulling and calling us all to turn and accept your love rather than to
follow our own ways. Go with us and be with us we ask
in the name of our Christ. Amen.

CHAPTER 2. HEATHENISM, INDIANS, AND CHRISTIANITY

1. What does Wesley mean by the term "Heathen"?

2. How does Wesley use the term "atheist"?

3. What are the "idols" Wesley says are common to atheism?

4. How and why did Wesley's view of the "noble savage" change?

5. How does Wesley think that Heathens can be saved?

6. In what ways does Wesley think Heathens fall short of Christianity?

NOTES

SCRIPTURE

For I am not ashamed of the gospel; it is the power of God for salvation to everyone who has faith, to the Jew first and also to the Greek. For in it the righteousness of God is revealed through faith for faith; as it is written, "The one who is righteous will live by faith."

ROMANS 1:16–17

PRAYER

Almighty God, father of Abraham, Isaac, and Joseph; who called your people out of the land of their captivity in Egypt, we give you praise. You have made covenant after covenant with the people you have called out of your boundless love to be your people. We have not always answered that call, we have not always followed your will, we have preferred and thought our way was better, and for these things forgive us. We give thanks for your continued seeking after us with your love.
Be with us now and bless us in the name of your Son our Lord,
Jesus Christ. Amen.

CHAPTER 3. JUDAISM AND CHRISTIANITY

1. In what two categories does Wesley divide the Jews? What is the basis of this division?

2. What is the Jewish Dispensation?

3. What failures does Wesley find in the Jews?

4. By what method or in what way are the Jews able to be saved?

5. What does Wesley believe about the final resolution of the Jews to God?

6. What does Wesley mean by saying that the Jew is in a spirit of bondage?

NOTES

SCRIPTURE

My point is this: heirs, as long as they are minors, are no better than slaves, though they are the owners of all the property; but they remain under guardians and trustees until the date set by the father. So with us; while we were minors, we were enslaved to the elemental spirits, we were enslaved to the elemental spirits of the world. But when the fullness of time had come, God sent his Son, born of a woman, born under the law, in order to redeem those who were under the law, so that we might receive adoption as children. And because you are children, God has sent the Spirit of his Son into our hearts, crying, "Abba! Father!" So you are no longer a slave but a child, and if a child then also an heir, through God.

GALATIANS 4:1–7

PRAYER

Father of our Lord Jesus Christ we are thankful for our ability to gather together and share our thoughts and ideas with one another. We are thankful that you sent your Son into the world to reveal your love for us, and the mighty miracle that you are the Creator God and also the Redeemer God. Bless our deliberations and time together we ask in the name of our Christ. Amen.

CHAPTER 4. DEISM AND "TRUE CHRISTIANITY"

1. How would you describe Deism?

2. What does the Deist believe about God?

3. How does the Deist handle the two areas of knowledge: reason and revelation?

4. What failures does Wesley find in Deism? Who would you consider to be modern Deists?

5. What does Wesley think about the possibility of salvation for the Deist?

6. What are the positions of the Deist and the "True Christian" concerning the Order of Salvation?

7. Discuss the doctrine of the Atonement as the main problem area between the Deist and the Christian.

NOTES

SCRIPTURE

For just as the body is one and has many members, and all the members of the body, though many, are one body, so it is with Christ. For in the one Spirit we were all baptized into one body—Jews or Greeks, slaves or free—and we were all made to drink of one Spirit.

1 CORINTHIANS 12:12–13

PRAYER

Heavenly Father, who has loved us when we were most contentious, when we were most unlovable, when we fought and struggled against your will, we give thanks for your forgiving love found by faith in your Son, Jesus the Christ. Help us to study together and learn more about your love for us for we ask it in the name of Jesus. Amen.

CHAPTER 5. ROMAN CATHOLICISM
AND "TRUE CHRISTIANITY"

1. What does Wesley think about the persecution and abuse of the Roman Catholic?

2. What does Wesley mean by the terms *opinions* and *doctrines*?

3. How does Wesley relate religion with opinions?

4. Wesley is known for saying that if our hearts are the same give me your hand. What does he mean by this?

5. How do Wesley and the Roman Catholics differ in regard to the sacraments?

6. From Wesley's point of view, can a Roman Catholic be saved?

7. Discuss some of the issues/problems Wesley has with the Roman Catholic versus "True Christianity."

NOTES

SCRIPTURE

For I received from the Lord what I also handed on to you, that the Lord Jesus on the night when he was betrayed took a loaf of bread, and when he had given thanks, he broke it and said, "This is my body that is for you. Do this in remembrance of me." In the same way he took the cup also, after supper, saying, "This cup is the new covenant in my blood. Do this, as often as you drink it, in remembrance of me." For as often as you eat this bread and drink the cup, you proclaim the Lord's death until he comes.

1 CORINTHIANS 11:23–26

PRAYER

Most gracious Heavenly Father, we give thanks to you for your great mercies. We sing praises to you, we open our hearts to you, and we try to glorify your name. We give thanks for the Supper of our Lord that He gave to us before He was crucified for our sins. Bless and be with us as we study together to learn more about your love for us.
In Christ's name we ask it. Amen.

CHAPTER 6. QUAKERISM AND "TRUE CHRISTIANITY"

1. What differences do Wesley and the Quakers have concerning the value of private revelation, reason, and the Scriptures?

2. What problem does Wesley have with the way Quakers use *works*?

3. How do Wesley and the Quakers differ in their concept of the sacraments?

4. What does Wesley mean when he says Quaker doctrines might be in error but the Quakers might still have the reality of religion?

5. What does Wesley think about the possibility of salvation for the Quakers?

6. Explain the differences Wesley finds between Quakerism and "True Christianity."

NOTES

SCRIPTURE

There is one body and one Spirit, just as you were called to the one hope of your calling, one Lord, one faith, one baptism, one God and Father of all, who is above all and through all and in all.

Eᴘʜᴇsɪᴀɴs 4:4–6

PRAYER

We give thanks to you our Father God that you have sent your Son into the world for us. We are thankful for the church universal which the Son and the Holy Spirit have created in this world and are still working through until the end of time. Bless our church community, our love for each other, and our willingness to share our thoughts and ourselves with each other all in the love that proceeds from you, Oh God. Bless our studies together in the name of our Christ. Amen.

CHAPTER 7. MYSTICISM AND "TRUE CHRISTIANITY"

1. How does Wesley understand the term "Mystic" in his day?

2. What is Wesley's argument with the Mystics about the means of grace?

3. Describe the problems that Wesley finds with *solitary religion*.

4. How does Wesley state the case for reason as opposed by the Mystics?

5. What did Wesley think about the Mystics' use of Scripture?

6. Wesley believes the Mystics wrongheaded, but what allows him to say that the Mystic can be saved?

NOTES

SCRIPTURE

*Now the Lord said to Abram, "Go from your country and your kindred
and your father's house to the land that I will show you. I will make of you
a great nation, and I will bless you, and make your name great, so that you
will be a blessing. I will bless those who bless you, and the one who curses
you I will curse; and in you all the families of the earth shall be blessed."
So Abram went, as the Lord had told him;*

GENESIS 12:1–4A

PRAYER

Our Father, who in love has called us, may we respond like Abram of old.
When he was told to move from his country to another, he went. May
we, when we hear your call, be willing to move from our comfortable
ways, and locations, and move about doing your will as did Abram. We
thank you for this time we have had together to share in love our studies
and thoughts. Bless us as we go forth from this place that we might go
where you have led us. In the name of our Christ. Amen.

CHAPTER 8. CONCLUSION

1. How would you describe Wesley's view of Christianity and what he
   calls "True Christianity"?

2. How does Wesley's view of prevenient grace relate to our thinking
   about other religions?

3. How did Wesley argue against what he considered the corruptions of Christianity?

4. What does Wesley mean when he says he believes in salvation by faith and not salvation by doctrine?

NOTES

Answers to Chapter Questions

INTRODUCTION

1. To find out if Wesley thinks all religions are the same or if there is a uniqueness in Christianity; to see what Wesley thinks about some others who consider themselves Christian, but are very different; and to see if it is possible for people in either or both of these groups to be saved. (p. viii)

2. Heathenism, Judaism, Roman Catholicism, Deism, Mysticism, and Quakerism are the "isms." (p. xiv)

3. Wesley's writings as found in his "works," "letters," "journals," "notes," and "hymns." (p. xiv–xv)

4. A doctrine states a *fact*, (i.e. what the doctrine is about). The *manner* of a doctrine is how that fact came into existence, or how it is described. An example would be the doctrine of the Incarnation. The doctrine is that Jesus was both wholly God and wholly man. This we know, but to say how or in what *manner* this can be accomplished is beyond us; it is a mystery. Another example would be the Creation. The doctrine is that God is the creator; that is the *fact*. How He creates or the *manner* in which He creates is something that we do not know. (p. xvi)

5. A *doctrine* is defined in the same way as in the previous question. In this case *right opinions* or *orthodoxy* are used to interpret the doctrine. An excellent example is the doctrine of the Atonement. The *doctrine* of the Atonement is that God was reconciling the world to Himself through Christ dying on the cross. However, the theory of how this reconciliation comes about or why Christ had to die for it to affect our salvation is a matter of opinion. There are at least three main Christian views or theories of how the atonement works. Wesley said he didn't know and didn't think anybody else knew exactly how it worked. Any "how" would be a matter of *opinion*. (p. xvi)

6. The first definition "everything in the relationship between God and man that comes from God's grace" includes *prevenient grace* and in fact spends much time in discussing *prevenient grace*. The

second definition is limited to two concepts: *justification* and *sanctification*. *Justification* means our pardon or forgiveness of sins and *sanctification* means the process of growth in holiness from justification to perfection. (p. xvii)

7. Charles Wesley wrote over 6,000 hymns. John Wesley wanted to teach his new converts about Christianity. They would probably not long remember his preached words but they would better remember Charles's words set to the tunes of the day. In this way John reached the uneducated masses. Even today *The United Methodist Hymnal* is full of theology. (p. xviii)

CHAPTER 1. NATURAL MAN AND PREVENIENT GRACE

1. Wesley believes the Image of God to be made up of three elements: *natural image, political image,* and *moral image.* The natural image and political image have become distorted and twisted from their original state, however some remnants are still left in man. The moral image, on the other hand, has been lost. There is nothing we can do to restore it. It requires something outside and beyond us to restore the moral image. It requires God. (pp. 1–2)

2. Natural Man cannot be saved. He is spiritually bankrupt, asleep, and separated from the source or author of his salvation. (p. 3)

3. Natural Man, as Wesley describes him, does not exist. Natural Man is a logical abstraction. (pp. 3–4)

4. Wesley believed that the Garden of Eden and Adam and Eve's life, including Adam eating the forbidden fruit that caused man to fall into sin, was a historical reality. More scholars today doubt the historicity but not the important religious significance of the Garden of Eden. (p. 4)

5. Wesley has two definitions of sin. The first is an inclination to evil and in which the faculties of man have been twisted, distorted, and perverted. The second is a total corruption of our human nature as God created it. In other words man is separated from God and man is unable within himself to better his condition within the Order of Salvation. The Order of Salvation is the process of man's salvation which beings with prevenient grace, then to the repentance of man and justifying grace, then sanctifying grace, and then the final end things, which are heaven and the afterlife. (pp. 4–5)

6. Wesley believes that though man is in a fallen condition, he still has some remnants left in the areas of personal talents, mental capacities, physical possibilities, and political or social works. He obviously has capacities in the arts, such as music, painting, sculpture, etc. In the natural and political image man can do many talented and good things, however in the moral image, the relationship with God, man can do nothing but wait upon God's prior action. Without God's act, man is morally bankrupt, separated from God and unable to do anything to save himself. (p. 6)

7. Wesley states that prevenient grace is the preventing grace given by God to every man. It is the grace of God that calls forth the good desires that arise in us. It is also the first stirrings within us to know more about Him, to consider prayer or reading of Scripture, to learn more about Him, or our first thoughts about God. (pp. 8–11)

8. Wesley considers conscience to be a part of the prevenient grace of God. The uneasy feelings we may have when we do something that is not in line with our conscience is believed to be the prevenient grace of God. (pp. 8–9)

9. By having the doctrine of prevenient grace—God making the first move towards man, towards reconciliation—Wesley is able to charge man with either accepting this grace or rejecting this grace. The grace of God is freely given but man must choose to accept the grace in order to complete the reconciliation. If man had no choice, as we find in predestination, the doctrine of prevenient grace would have no place and the resulting necessity of man choosing to accept or reject the grace of God would not apply. (pp. 11–16)

10. Because God has taken the first step in the reconciliation process by giving to all mankind his prevenient grace, man cannot take total responsibility for his salvation. There is no "work" to it, man is free to accept or reject the grace that God has already freely given him. Though man must respond to complete the process of reconciliation, man could not even accept God's grace unless God had already given it to him. (pp. 9–11)

11. Man is responsible for his salvation only in the sense that he has to accept God's gift. Unless man accepts the gift he is not reconciled, but if he accepts God's prior gift he is reconciled. Thus man is responsible, but he can only be responsible because God has made

the first move. Again, as Wesley said, "by the grace of God we may cast away all our transgressions. Therefore, if we do not want, they are chargeable on ourselves. We *may* live; but we *will* die." (pp. 12–16)

CHAPTER 2. HEATHENISM, INDIANS, AND CHRISTIANITY

1. Wesley considers a Heathen as a non-Christian. The term "Heathen" did not carry all of the negative baggage it has collected since then. In fact, Wesley does not distinguish between the term "Heathen" and others such as atheism, infidel, dissipation, and in some cases even Indian. (pp. 17–18)

2. Dissipation and atheist are basically the same for him. He does not believe that the usual definition of atheist as one who does not believe in God is correct. In his experience Wesley says he has hardly found such a person. He defines atheism as a practical atheist, meaning a person who has no thought or who does not think about God or have fellowship with Him. (pp. 17–19)

3. "Desire of the eye" or what appeals to the imagination. "Pride of life," which seeks happiness in the praises of men. "Love of money" when used for its own end. "Idolizing a human creature" by putting the creature in the place of the Creator—God. (pp. 20–22)

4. Before Wesley went to America he was caught up in the idea of the "noble savage." He anticipated that they would be open to the gospel and even ready to teach him. He, like many of his contemporaries in Europe, expected them to be free from all of the errors and sins found in Europe at the time. Europeans were writing about the "noble savage" in the abstract—they had never met one. After Wesley met some Indians in America, and especially after he talked to some of the traders who dealt with them and had no reason to speak kindly, he changed his mind about them. Wesley was sorely disappointed because rather than being open to his gospel, they were not; rather than being without the perceived sins of modern Europe, they had their own sins. That, along with the information he received from the traders, prejudiced as it was, did not square with his preconceived notions. (pp. 23–26)

5. Wesley pleaded ignorance on this question. He also said that the Heathen cannot be excluded from salvation and that if saved it

would be due to their sincerity. The Heathen would be saved by the grace of God. (p. 26)

6. Wesley thinks that the Heathens fall short in many ways. They have a religion of externals whereas Christianity is a religion of the heart. They lack the Christian truths of the Incarnation and the Holy Spirit. Especially do they not have the doctrine of Original Sin, the sin of Adam and Eve in eating the fruit of the tree of knowledge of good and evil. (pp. 28–30)

CHAPTER 3. JUDAISM AND CHRISTIANITY

1. The two categories are the Jews who lived before Christ and those who lived after Christ. Jews who live after Christ live after the work God performed through His Son. (pp. 35–36)

2. The Jewish Dispensation means that the Jews entered into a relationship with God. In this relationship was the ritual law. This dispensation involved God's work through Moses and the deliverance of the people from the land of Egypt. (pp. 38–40)

3. The basic failure is that the Jews fail to leave their old dispensation and enter the new one that God gave to man through Christ. He also charges them with making religion one of meat and drink and not righteousness, peace, and joy. You could therefore say that they were not true to the requirements of their own dispensation because their religion is too external and not internal enough. (pp. 40–43)

4. Wesley believes the Jew, like the Christian, will be saved by faith. The Jews' faith is in the Jewish dispensation and the God of that dispensation. (pp. 44–45)

5. Wesley believes that at some point the Jews will come back into the saving relationship with God. They will return when the full quota of Gentiles have been brought in to the fellowship with God. Wesley believes that at some point the Jews would return to the complete fold of God. This is to occur after the quota of Gentiles has been brought into that same fellowship. (p. 46)

6. The Jew has the fear of God and the law, which shows man his sin. They do not have the depth of the relationship with God that God has given the Christian. (pp. 49–50)

CHAPTER 4. DEISM AND "TRUE CHRISTIANITY"

1. Deism was an attempt to water down or reduce the specific beliefs of religion so that all men could agree with their concepts. Lord Herbert of Cherbury gave five points that were pretty common among Deists of the day. (The points are: 1. Belief in one supreme God. 2. This supreme God is the one who ought to be worshipped by all men. 3. The two chief parts of worshipping this God are virtue and piety. 4. We ought to be sorry for the sins that we have committed, and repent of them. 5. The goodness of God relates to man by His giving rewards and punishments to men, both in this life and the life to come.) (pp. 51–52)

2. Yes, the Deist believes in God but the god he believes in is quite different from the Christian God. Also, the Christian uses the means of grace but the Deist may or may not. (pp. 52–53)

3. Deists relied on reason to make their case and to seek adherents. They had no use for revelation at all. It is difficult to make a religion of reason and to have every one agree to it. (pp. 57–61)

4. Deists tend to reason further than reason can really take them. At some point there has to be faith or a revelation that is basic and behind the reasoning process. There has to be something taken in faith for a rational argument to take place. Perhaps this is one reason why Deism as a philosophy has pretty well disappeared. William Law, for one, did not agree that God is omnipotent. They deny the justice of God by denying the wrath of God. For Wesley the Bible is basic and for Law and the Deists, reason is basic. (pp. 57–61)

5. Wesley thinks that the Deist should continue to press on in their faith until they become a full Christian. The Deist is a *servant* of God or in the spirit of bondage rather than a *son* of God. Wesley would never condemn any man; he leaves that up to God. He is able to find some good in all of those he opposes and always leaves the door open to the possibility of salvation for any man regardless of the religious misconceptions they may hold. (pp. 57–60)

6. The Deist believed that Jesus came to teach men the moral law. If that law is broken one must feel sorry and change their behavior. Wesley believed that Christ is more than a teacher of law; He is the savior of mankind. Jesus came into the world to bear the sins of the world and thereby to bring God and man back together in a relationship of love. To summarize, in the Order of Salvation,

the Deist had little to offer but a system of morals. Wesley had the possibility of salvation through the mighty work of God through His Son. (p. 65)

7. The Deist did not believe in the Christian doctrine of Atonement, whereas for Wesley it was a vital part of Christianity. If Jesus was only a teacher of morality he certainly could not be the savior and for Wesley He was the savior. (pp. 63–67)

CHAPTER 5. ROMAN CATHOLICISM AND "TRUE CHRISTIANITY"

1. Wesley did not think that Catholics should be persecuted. He thought that they were in the Catholic Church, the worldwide church, and as such should be greeted as a Christian rather than persecuted as a non-Christian. (pp. 68–69)

2. *Opinions* are of lesser value than *doctrines*. Doctrines are basic Christian beliefs and must be believed by all Christians. However, as the doctrine is further explained it can become an opinion and when that happens good Christians may disagree on them. Doctrines are basic and opinions are further explanations of the doctrines. (pp. 57–61)

3. Religion and opinions are two entirely different things. Religion is a vital, living relationship with God. Opinions are ideas about that religion, explanations of that religion. (pp. 70–71)

4. Wesley's "hand" was given only after the parties had gone a long way towards unity. This meant that their heart and mind must be right with God, they must believe in Christ (that He is God), have a faith filled with love, must not be a Quietist but use their life in stewardship, render service to God, love all mankind, and love God and neighbor by doing good works. If all this is agreed to, then Wesley is ready to give his hand. (pp. 70–72)

5. Wesley believes in two sacraments and the Roman Catholics believe in seven. He believes in the once and single sacrifice of Jesus Christ whereas the Roman church believes in a sacrifice at each mass. Wesley also points out that no work of man can bring about our salvation, emphasizing that justification is by grace alone, by faith alone. Whereas the Catholics believe that one should participate with God by performing works to help qualify them for the grace of God, Wesley believes that all is from God and that

our good words come after justification, not before. (pp. 75–79, 87–88)

6. Wesley believes that Roman Catholics certainly can be saved. They have all of the faith that they need, even though their church has doctrines, sacraments, and practices that are more than what is needed. Wesley would not deny any Roman Catholic salvation based on his being a Roman Catholic. (pp. 80–83)

7. Obviously, Wesley does not give the preeminence to the Pope that the Catholics do. Likewise the Roman Catholic Church is not the only Catholic Church, there are others. The fact that the Romans have made additions to the sacraments is well known. Wesley particularly had trouble with the doctrine of penance. For Wesley, the sacraments are vehicles of the grace of God, and this, for him, is more important than trying to make a distinction between the matter and form of the sacrament. For instance, in the Lord's Supper the matter is the bread and wine (grape juice) and the form is the words of consecration. (pp. 83–93)

CHAPTER 6. QUAKERISM AND "TRUE CHRISTIANITY"

1. The Quakers believe that the Scriptures are on a par or equal to private revelation. Wesley believes that the Scriptures are primary and that private revelation must be checked by the Scriptures. (p. 95)

2. Wesley believes that Quakerism tends to lead to justification by works rather than justification by faith. Wesley's earliest years bordered on works rather than faith. He thought that he had to perform, to do good works, and was a part of the "Holy Club" at Oxford, so called because of the rigorous scheduling of their activities. Later he realized that justification is a gift of God's grace and not something that man can do to influence the good will of God towards him. (pp. 97–98)

3. The Quakers do not require the use of the sacraments. Wesley believes the sacraments are means of God's grace that we are to use because they may well be the channels by which God gives us preventing, justifying, or sanctifying grace. (pp. 99–101)

4. Wesley is saying that Quakers might be wrong in their doctrines but that does not mean that they cannot be partakers of true reli-

gion. They may be confused in their doctrines but if they have the
reality of religion, they may be saved. (pp. 103–4)

5. Wesley thinks that they are wrong in their doctrines but they may
still have the reality of a true relationship with God and that is
more vital and meaningful than our expression of that relationship. Wesley, therefore opens the door to the Quakers having the
true religion experience, but having poorly stated that experience.
(pp. 103–5)

6. Wesley has problems with the Quaker use of the Scriptures because they allow private revelations at times to be on a par with
or maybe superior to the Scriptures. He is strong on justification
by faith rather than works, but he does push for works after justification. He also believes that the Quakers allow too much for the
outer conditions of worship to be superior to the inner experience. Finally, he strongly believes in the means of grace (Scripture
reading, prayer, and sacraments) and their importance for us. (pp.
105–10)

CHAPTER 7. MYSTICISM AND "TRUE CHRISTIANITY"

1. Wesley found that there were about as many definitions of
Mysticism as there were those who thought they were Mystics.
They likewise seemed to reach for the ends of religion without using the means of religion. Obviously since many of them thought
that they should passively wait for the moving of the Holy Spirit,
without any personal effort toward moral striving or use of the
church as an institution, Wesley saw them as seeking the ends
without the means. (pp. 112–14)

2. Since many of the Mystics thought the means of grace were not for
everybody, Wesley would disagree. He believes that public prayer,
Scripture, the Lord's Supper, and Christian Perfection are for everybody. (pp. 127–28)

3. Wesley believes that there is no such thing as *solitary religion*. To be
Christian or indeed, religious, means that we have to be in a group
of those likeminded. Jesus started the church with His disciples
and from that time onward Christianity was a group, a church, a
way, not for the individual but for the group. (pp. 128–29)

4. Wesley believes that the Mystics are very wrong with their denial
of reason. Reason is very import for the believing person. We are

to use reason as best we can. In order to lay the foundation of religion, people must use reason. We cannot work out inner or outer holiness without reason. (pp. 122–26)

5. The Mystics have their own experiences, which they believe are primary even when they differ from Scripture. Wesley believes that we should test these experiences against the Scripture because for him the Scripture is primary. They sometimes want to have their religion and experiences apart from the church as an institution. Wesley believes that a Christian should be in the church since Christ started the Church and is in the church, the Holy Spirit works in the church, and the means of grace are found in the church and in the life of the Christian. (pp. 122–26)

6. Again, Wesley thinks that they are very wrongheaded, but they may have the true Christian experience as well. He is not willing to say they cannot be saved merely because their doctrine is incorrect. (pp. 125–26)

CHAPTER 8. CONCLUSION

1. Wesley seeks an intimate, personal, dynamic relationship between God and man, made possible by Christ. This relationship has the Scripture as its authority, aided by the reason of man. (pp. 133–35)

2. Prevenient grace is basic to Wesley's thoughts on those who believe other religions. No man is able to live apart from the grace of God and the first part of that grace is the prevenient grace of God. Prevenient grace is the preventing grace given by God to every man. It is the grace of God that calls forth the good desires that arise in us. It is also the first stirrings within us to know more about Him, to consider prayer or reading of Scripture, to learn more about Him, or our first thoughts about God. God is no respecter of persons; He loves everybody and wants everybody to love Him. (pp. 135–40)

3. Wesley uses the primary source of the Scripture and the secondary source of reason to combat all of the corruptions he found. He refuses to condemn his opponents because he believes that they will be held accountable to God and that is beyond Wesley. Though they have opinions extremely wide of the mark, he still believes they can be saved. (pp. 140–43)

4. Salvation by faith is primary and it is the faith in Christ, the faith in God, the reliance upon God, and our relationship with God and with our fellow man. It does not matter if we may have gotten the doctrine wrong or have been mislead. Fortunately it is our relationship with God that is primary and not our ability to reason or to describe that relationship. (pp. 142–43)

Bibliography

PRIMARY WORKS

Burtner, Robert W., and Robert E. Chiles. *A Compend of Wesley's Theology*. New York, NY: Abingdon Press, 1954. There are introductions to each area of Wesley's thought and then quotations are given from Wesley. This is a helpful, short, and interesting volume, especially for those who are new to the study of Wesley.

Wesley, John. *The Christian's Pattern*. Salem, OH: Schmul Publishing Co., 1975. This is John Wesley's extract of *The Imitation of Christ* by Thomas à Kempis.

———. *Explanatory Notes upon the New Testament*. London, England: The Epworth Press, 1954. First published in 1755. Valuable comments on the New Testament that any Methodist would find helpful, but you don't have to be a Methodist to appreciate these comments, as they are pretty solid.

———. *The Heart of John Wesley's Journal*. Edited by Percy Livingstone Parker. New York, NY: Methodist Book Concern, 1916? Very readable one volume condensed journal with excellent introductory material. Well worth the read.

———. *The Journal of John Wesley*. Edited by Nehemiah Curnock. A Bicentenary Issue, 8 vols. London, England: The Epworth Press, 1931. Fascinating reading about the daily thoughts and activities of John Wesley.

———. *Letters*. Edited by John Telford. 8 vols., 1st ed. London, England: 1931. The letters make interesting reading on many topics.

———. *Sermons By The Rev. John Wesley: Adapted to the Use of Students by Rev. W. P. Harrison*. Nashville, TN: Publishing House of the Methodist Episcopal Church, South, 1911. This book gives interesting introduction to the sermons of John Wesley. Students of the topic will find it useful.

———. *The Standard Sermons of John Wesley*. Edited by Edwin H. Sugden. 4th annotated ed. London, England: The Epworth Press, 1955. These two volumes of sermons are excellent reading. Although they are presented as sermons, many of them were well written presentations of Wesley's thoughts upon the subject.

———. *Wesley's Hymns*. London, England: John Mason, 1779. Interesting reading for the various hymns topics and the poetry of both John and Charles Wesley.

———. *Wesley's Notes on the Bible*. Edited by G. Roger Schoenhals. Grand Rapids, MI: Francis Asbury Press, 1987. Wesley's multi-volume *Notes on the Old Testament* is also available but this is a one volume set which includes portions of Wesley's comments on both the Old and New Testaments.

———. *The Works of John Wesley*. Edited by Thomas Jackson. 14 vols., 3rd ed. Grand Rapids, MI: Zondervan Publishing House, 1958–59. This is the first complete unabridged edition in nearly 100 years reproduced from the 1872 authorized edition and it contains an abundance of John's writings.

Wesley, John, and John Fletcher. *Entire Sanctification: Attainable in this Life*. Salem, OH: Schmul Publishing Co., date unknown. John Fletcher was one of John Wesley's preachers and an excellent theologian in his own right. Even though it is a little difficult to read, this is an interesting publication about Christian perfection. It is one of the most complete statements on Christian perfection that I have read. Paragraphs are numbered and there is a long question and answer section.

SECONDARY SOURCES

The Book of Discipline of the United Methodist Church. Nashville, TN: The United Methodist Publishing House, 2004. Any recent *Discipline* will have the theology of the United Methodist Church in them. Disciplines before the Methodist Church became united will also have the same theology that was given to the church by John Wesley.

Cannon, William R. *The Theology of John Wesley*. New York, NY: Abingdon Press, 1946. Dr. Cannon gives a very capable and readable theology of John Wesley.

Chilcote, Paul W., ed. *Wesleyan Tradition: a Paradigm for Renewal*. Nashville, TN: Abingdon Press, 2002. This is a good book, containing worthwhile material, but is not for the timid reader.

Collins, Kenneth J., and John H. Tyson. *Conversion in the Wesleyan Tradition*. Nashville, TN: Abingdon Press, 2001. This is an interesting book, but difficult for the average layperson to read.

Daniels, W. H. *The Illustrated History of Methodism in Great Britain and America: From the Days of the Wesleys to the Present Time*. New York, NY: Methodist Book Concern, 1879.

Davey, Cyril. *John Wesley and the Methodists*. Nashville, TN: Abingdon Press, 1985. This is a small book that has lots of excellent pictures. It contains some good information and is very readable.

Eldridge, Charles O. *A Popular Exposition of Methodist Theology*. Salem, OH: Schmul Publishing Co., reprint 1982. Original date unknown. This is a good book that the layperson will find easy to read.

Forsyth, P. T. *The Person and Place of Jesus Christ*. Congregational Union Lecture, 1909. London, England: Whales/Hodder & Stoughton, 1909. Forsyth was able to say things in an excellent manner. It is too bad that most of his books are extremely hard to find.

Green, Vivian. *John Wesley and Oxford*. Oxford, England: Thomas-Photos, 1979. A very easy booklet to read, containing many pictures and some information about John when he was at Oxford.

Harper, Steve. *John Wesley's Message For Today*. Grand Rapids, MI: Zondervan Publishing House, 1983. This is a very readable, but solid, book for the layperson.

Hildebrandt, Franz. *Christianity According to the Wesleys*. London, England: The Epworth Press, 1956. These are the Harris Franklin Rall Lectures of 1954 delivered at Garrett Biblical Institute, Evanston, Illinois. This book contains solid material but remains a readable book.

Hurst, John Fletcher. *The History of Methodism*. 6 vols. New York, NY: Eaton & Mains, 1902. Undoubtedly out of print, but has some good material in it.

Hyde, A. B. *The Story of Methodism*. Greenfield, MA: Willey & Co., 1887. Probably out of print by now but an interesting book for those who like to read the history.

James, William. *The Varieties of Religious Experience: A Study in Human Nature.* New York, NY: Modern Library, 1994. This is a classic that I am glad to say is still around and may be purchased at many bookstores.

Job, Rueben P. *A Wesleyan Spiritual Reader.* Nashville, TN: Abingdon Press, 1998. A Methodist Bishop uses Wesley as a basis for devotional readings. This is a very readable book with lots of good material. The layperson will have no difficulty with this one.

————. *Three Simple Rules: A Wesleyan Way of Living.* Nashville, TN: Abingdon Press, 2007. Bishop Rueben takes the rules of Wesley and elaborates upon them for the modern reader. This book is worthwhile and is very readable for the layperson.

Klaiber, Walter, and Manfred Marquardt. *Living Grace: An Outline of United Methodist Theology.* Translated by J. Steven O'Malley and Ulrike R. M. Guthrie. Nashville, TN: Abingdon Press, 2001. Tough sledding to read through this book for a layperson as it is written for those familiar with theology.

Latourette, Kenneth Scott. *A History of Christianity.* New York, NY: Harper & Brothers, 1953. Though a classic and very long, over 1400 pages, it is shorter than many others. Well written.

Lee, Umphrey. *John Wesley and Modern Religion.* Nashville, TN: Cokesbury, 1936. This is a readable book about John Wesley. It is difficult to find but worth the search.

Lindstrom, Harald. *Wesley and Sanctification.* 1950. Reprint, London, England: The Epworth Press, 1956. An excellent study in this topic, but perhaps not the easiest for the layperson.

Maddox, Randy L., et al. *Rethinking Wesley's Theology for Contemporary Methodism.* Nashville, TN: Kingswood Books, 1998. Due to the topic it is an interesting book. However it is difficult for the average layperson.

McConnell, Francis J. *John Wesley.* New York, NY: Abingdon Press, 1939. Very readable volume about the life of John Wesley and some of his thoughts. Worth the read.

McNeer, May, and Lynd Ward. *John Wesley.* Nashville, TN: Abingdon-Cokesbury Press, 1951. This is a small, very easy to read book that gives some of the history of John.

Nagler, Arthur W. *The Church in History.* New York, NY: Abingdon Press, 1929. Worth the read.

Neve, J. L. *A History of Christian Thought.* 2 vols. Philadelphia, PA: Muhlenberg Press, 1946. Excellent history that is readable. This book is undoubtedly out of date now.

Norwood, Frederick A. *The Development of Modern Christianity since 1500.* New York, NY: Abingdon Press, 1956. A good, short history that is readable.

Nygren, Anders. *Agape and Eros.* Translated by Philip S. Watson. London, England: S.P.C.K. Press, 1957. An excellent study of these two words that are so basic to Christianity.

Perkins, Barbara, et al. *Benet's Reader's Encyclopedia of American Literature.* New York, NY: HarperCollins Publishers, 1991.

Pollock, John. *John Wesley.* Wheaton, IL: Victor Books, 1989. A very readable and interesting book, mainly about Wesley's life.

Rattenbury, J. Ernest. *The Eucharistic Hymns of John and Charles Wesley.* London, England: The Epworth Press, 1948. A very able presentation for those interested in the hymns of the Wesleys, particularly those about Holy Communion.

————. *The Evangelical Doctrines of Charles Wesley's Hymns.* 3rd ed. London, England: The Epworth Press, 1954. An excellent work on the doctrines found within the Wesleyan hymns.

———. *Wesley's Legacy to the World.* London, England: The Epworth Press, 1938. Well done and very organized approach to the topics. It is a readable book for the non scholar.

Todd, John M. *John Wesley and the Catholic Church.* London, England: Hodder and Stoughton, 1958. Written by a Catholic, it is an interesting interpretation of John Wesley. Shows how Wesley can be used for the ecumenical work of the church.

The United Methodist Hymnal. Nashville, TN: The United Methodist Publishing House, 1992.

Watkins, W. T. *Out of Aldersgate.* Nashville, TN: Dept. of Education and Promotion, Board of Missions, Methodist Episcopal Church, South, 1937.

Watson, Philip S. *The Message of the Wesleys.* Grand Rapids, MI: Zondervan Publishing House, 1984. Has introductory comments by Watson and then quotes Wesley. A good read for the interested layperson.

Watson, Richard. *The Life of the Rev. John Wesley.* Translated and noted by John Emory. New York, NY: B. Waugh & T. Mason, 1832. This obviously is an old book, probably out of print, but it is very readable and well worth the time needed to read it.

Wellman, Sam. *John Wesley, Founder of the Methodist Church.* Uhrichsville, OH: Barbour Publishing Inc., 1997. Extremely readable; covers mainly his life but not much of his thought.

The Wesley Orders of Common Prayer. Edited by Edward C. Hobbs. Nashville, TN: Board of Education of the Methodist Church: 1957. This is a useful book for the layperson.

Williams, Colin W. *John Wesley's Theology Today.* New York, NY: Abingdon Press, 1955. A must read book for one seeking to understand the order of salvation by Wesley. It is also written with an eye to the ecumenical movement.

Wood, Allan W. "Deism." In *Encyclopedia of Religion*, 2nd ed., 2251. Detroit, MI: Macmillan, 2005.

www.ingramcontent.com/pod-product-compliance
Lightning Source LLC
Chambersburg PA
CBHW060339100426
42812CB00003B/1048